THE
BRAND
WHO CRIED "WOLF"

THE
BRAND
WHO CRIED "WOLF"

DELIVER ON YOUR COMPANY'S PROMISE
AND CREATE CUSTOMERS FOR LIFE

SCOTT DEMING

1807
WILEY
2007
BICENTENNIAL

John Wiley & Sons, Inc.

Published by John Wiley & Sons, Inc., Hoboken, New Jersey.
Published simultaneously in Canada.

For general information on our other products and services please contact our Customer Care Department within the United States at (800) 762-2974, outside the United States at (317) 572-3993 or fax (317) 572-4002.

Wiley also publishes its books in a variety of electronic formats. Some content that appears in print may not be available in electronic books.

Library of Congress Cataloging-in-Publication Data:

Deming, Scott.
    The brand who cried wolf : deliver on your company's promise and create customers for life / Scott Deming.
        p.   cm.
    ISBN 978-0-470-12712-4 (cloth)
        1. Brand name products.   2. Brand name products—Management.
    3. Success in business.   I. Title.
    HD69.B7D46   2007
    658.8'27—dc22

                                                                    2007002549

10   9   8   7   6   5   4   3   2   1

To my Dad—
Alden Lincoln Deming Jr.

Shortly before this book went to press, my Dad passed away on February 20, 2007. He was 72 years young. Dad was a man among men—war veteran, Marine, tough guy, spiritual beacon, teacher, and tender, loving, devoted family man. He was my mentor, my pal, my guide, my calm, my hero. My Dad was everything to me. The fact that he never had the opportunity to read this book makes me very sad, because his wisdom, guidance, and influence can be found throughout every page. I wanted so badly for him to see the culmination of his love and devotion. This book would not have been possible without him.

This is for you, Dad.

I love you and miss you more than I can possibly put into words.

CONTENTS

CONTENTS

CONTENTS

PREFACE

WHAT'S UP WITH THE CHILDREN'S STORIES?

No, you're not reading a children's book! But there are children's stories in it. That's because they're a fun and unique way to engage you in a new thinking style as we discover the *real* formula for personal and professional success.

When we were children, our parents read us bedtime stories full of sensational characters like talking animals, villains dressed up as trusted family members—the better to trick and deceive—and good, honest people who do the right thing. In each story, although the basic premise was to entertain, there was always a point: to teach us valuable life lessons and to groom us and shape our values by inculcating in us, among other things, beliefs about good conduct, citizenship, productivity, and relationships. Although such lessons were taught in myriad ways, from tough love punishment to lectures, to Sunday school, some of our most valuable and memorable lessons were delivered by our favorite children's stories. You still remember "The Three Little Pigs" and its lesson of working hard to build a strong house. And you still remember "The Tortoise and the Hare" and the lesson of diligence and persistence. And there is "The Goose That Laid the Golden Egg" and the lesson of never taking shortcuts to success. The list goes on and on.

Now as adults, we teach our own children most of the same lessons, and in many of the same ways. Not surprisingly, one of the most popular forms of teaching among all these techniques is still the story. And interestingly enough, the majority of the stories we read to our children today are the very same ones our parents read to us and their parents had read to them!

Children's fairy tales teach children how to live, and at the time, it all seemed so simple. So, what changes, as we become adults? We become engrained in our daily activities—our businesses, our various responsibilities. It's true that life becomes more complicated. Unfortunately, because of this adult, responsible, complex life we live, the wonderful and important lessons we learned at such an early age become diluted and go out of focus. As a result, we fail to heed these lessons even as we teach them to our own children.

But the truth in these stories hasn't changed, and there's no reason why we should, either. It is realistic—even necessary—to believe that the lessons learned from our most treasured childhood tales could help us to greatly improve our relationships, jobs, businesses, and brands. The enduring nature of these stories shows that there truly are only a few simple rules and values to adhere to that will help us live and serve in an appropriate, productive, profitable, and rewarding manner. I am not trivializing the importance of research, profit margins, sales goals, and attention to detail required for business success. I'm simply saying that focusing on the details day in, day out can easily cloud our vision and prevent us from seeing the bigger picture—and the direction for our lives. And it is in the bigger picture that these early-in-life lessons, these wonderful stories, lie.

CREATING BELIEFS THAT SHAPE YOUR BRAND!

The bigger picture—the connection between the values found in children's stories and branding—is a matter of belief. Everything in our lives, from our values to the choices we make about what products to buy, is guided by the beliefs we have. From the moment we're born, we begin experiencing the world. From these experiences we develop beliefs about who we are and how we want to be: In general, we develop values that shape our engagement with the world. When we believe that it's important to deliver on our promises, for example, part of what we're doing is staking a claim about how we think the world works, or how we *want* to see it work. When we believe keeping one's promises is valuable, this belief motivates us to act in a particular way. In fact, beliefs are what drive people's actions. What I show you in this book is how to create beliefs in the hearts, minds, and souls of your customers that are so incredibly strong, so full of conviction, that the customers are unwilling to part with them—and unwilling to part with you.

Although the processes whereby we form our beliefs are complicated, once a belief is fixed in our minds we're typically very unwilling to get rid of it. That's because we equate our beliefs with truth and reality. We're so committed to our beliefs we often cannot fathom that one or more of them could be wrong. Think about how we react to challenges to them. When someone tells us that what we believe is false, our first response is typically to reject the challenge out of hand. For example, people were initially resistant about accepting that their beliefs about the shape of Earth or its movement in relation to the sun were false.

It's no different in business. Consider how many people insist on following a certain business model even when it's been shown to be unprofitable. Beliefs are powerful, and they are motivating. We know that swift moving, get rich quick, poor planning models don't work. Yet companies like Pets.com do it anyway. That company attempted an immediate domination of the Internet market for pet supplies, and that's one of the reasons the company went bust. Consider, on the other hand, Amazon.com, which weathered the dot com bust. Though the company grew rapidly, founder Jeff Bezos' thinking was long term.

The comparison reminds me of the fable "The Tortoise and the Hare." Some beliefs about business models simply don't work over the long haul. If, for example, you believe in get rich quick schemes, and use them as your business model, you'll soon find that whatever money you have made quickly disappears. Remember the greedy couple who killed their golden goose? As we see in Chapter 3, it was *against* this sort of thinking that the founders of Google laid out their corporate mission when they took their company public. The firm belief that killing the golden goose would *not* be the best experience for anyone involved was their guiding principle. To date, Google has been a *very* successful brand.

Not only do we equate our beliefs with truth, we also equate them with goodness. Our beliefs are good because they're true. Therefore, our actions are based on the belief that what we do is good or will result in something good. Even when we do things that seem to contradict what's good for us, we do it with the belief that at least something about it is good. Believing that exercise is good seems to be contradicted by sitting on the couch instead of taking a jog. Yet we justify sitting on the couch based on the belief that it's good to rest. In this way, our belief—whatever it is at the moment—is a belief about truth *and* goodness.

My own dear mother is a perfect example of this idea. She has been smoking since she was thirteen years old. As this book goes to press, she is close to age seventy. She still smokes. Though it's true she's tried to quit a couple of times, deep down she truly believes it's okay to smoke—*she'll* be okay. She has many reasons to quit, from the medical evidence that smoking is linked to many diseases, but doesn't.

The same thing happens in business. Corporations do things that are unprofitable and unproductive, because it is part of their belief system that these things will work. They make decisions even in the face of evidence that it's not going to work, because their belief system is so strong. For example, some businesses believe that relying on technology (such as automated voice menus) instead of people to interact with customers is the right thing to do—no matter how many customers complain about how impersonal and ineffective technology can be.

The belief you have about the type of person you are is no less important to your business relationships than to your other, personal connections. And when you are working to create a brand, you are working to create a belief for your customers that they're extremely unwilling to part with—a belief that has lasting value. Creating beliefs in the hearts and minds of your customers about you, your company, your values—your *brand*—is the core element of success.

The Introduction provides us with a terrific starting point for understanding what branding is and why it matters to you!

ACKNOWLEDGMENTS

Within the pages of this book there is so much influence, inspiration, advice, collaboration, wisdom, friendship, love, and support from so many different people whom I wish to thank.

To my wife and life partner Debbie—Wow! We've been through it all. How can I ever thank you for the years of love and support? You have physically and emotionally held me up when I could not stand on my own. Your inner strength is unbelievable. I can't imagine doing any of it without you or being where I am right now if you weren't by my side. We are quite a team. I love you, my soul mate. To my children, who are truly the source of my dreams, drive, laughter, and inspiration, you are the reasons why the goofy little kid still lives inside me. Ryan, Danielle, Taylor, and Nicole, I am so very proud of you and I love you more than you'll ever know. I am your Faj! To my mom and dad, Doris and Al, the greatest parents ever to grace this planet, my rock and my foundation, whose guidance, values, encouragement, support, and unconditional love have made me the man I am today—who mean everything to me and whom I will always love so much. To my brothers Steve and Ken who always keep me in line. You remind me to keep it real and remember who I am and where I came from. We've laughed, cried, argued, and had each other's backs. I can't imagine three men being any closer. You are my best friends. Thank you for being there throughout the years. I love you both.

To my agent, Jackie Meyer of the Whimsy Literary Agency, who believed in me enough to work longer and harder than any person should have to. Thank you so much, Jackie, for your loyalty, guidance, honesty, dedication, and constant support and confidence. This would not have been possible without you. To my friend Mia Wood—your knowledge, wisdom, and words flow throughout this book. What a wonderful experience collaborating with you! Thank you for picking up the phone every time I called and being there when I needed you. You're the best! To all the wonderful people at John Wiley & Sons who worked extremely hard to make my dream and this book a reality. To Kim Dayman, Marketing Manager, who guided me through every stage of this project from book design to publicity. Your words of advice are priceless. To Tiffany Groglio, Editorial Assistant—I've never been around a more dedicated, buttoned-up, conscientious individual in my professional life. You make it happen! To Linda Witzling, Production Editor—thank you for working around my crazy schedule and bringing this book to market even sooner than I expected! To Richard Narramore, Senior Editor, who from day one showed genuine interest in me and my work and a sincere desire to make the book the best it could be. Richard, you're not just a pro, you're a great guy. Thank you.

ACKNOWLEDGMENTS

To the following individuals who have in some significant way inspired, educated, moved, and supported me during my life: Thank you, Greg Warmbrodt, Candace Beach, Barbara Mc-Murray, Joel Bauer, Larry Becker, Jane and John Stopher, Joe Zielinski, Bill Dando, Dr. Milton Richards, Joe DeLion, Vito Lupo, John Pullum, Ken Chandler, Wayne Irons, Jodie Noe Musselwhite, and my grandparents. Thank you, thank you, thank you.

INTRODUCTION

"THE BOY WHO CRIED 'WOLF'"

Once upon a time, there was a young boy who tended sheep up in the hills. It was solitary work, and with no one to play with, the boy grew lonely. So, one day he cried out, "Wolf! Wolf!" The entire population of the town came running to the hills to rescue the boy and protect the sheep. But when they arrived, there was no wolf. The boy fell down laughing, delighted that the townsfolk had come.

He thought it was a wonderful game and so played again the next day. "Wolf! Wolf!" came the horrible cry. Again, the townsfolk rushed to the hills, only to find, once again, no wolf. The sheep were grazing peacefully, and the shepherd boy once again squealed with glee.

Needless to say, the townsfolk were not at all happy. "Why should we believe him?" they grumbled. So, they resolved to ignore him when he played his trick again.

Unfortunately for the shepherd boy, wolves finally did sneak into the flock and attack the sheep. Terrified, the boy screamed, "Wolf! Wolf! Oh please come quickly, the wolves are eating all the sheep!"

Down in the town, the citizens heard the boy's desperate pleas, but they turned away. No matter how plaintive the boy's cries were, the townsfolk would not come to his aid, and the wolves took their leisure, eating every last sheep one by one.

The moral of the story: Don't say something if you don't mean it. Once you lose someone's trust, it's almost impossible to get it back!

The most successful relationships you and your organization have with other people are those built on trust. And a crucial component of earning the trust of others is acting on your word. Simple formula, isn't it? Making a promise plus keeping your promise equals trust. But let's take it a step further. Once you've earned someone's trust, you now have the opportunity to take that relationship to a whole new level, one that transcends what a typical relationship is. If you create memorable and unique experiences for your customers, and they trust you based on those experiences, they will become loyal to you and only you. Out of that loyalty, they will come to you again and again. Additionally, these same loyal customers will help you build your brand and your business because they will evangelize on your behalf. True. Creating unique, emotional, and memorable experiences turns a typical customer into a loyal, raving fan for life! And it is these loyal, raving fans, these evangelists, who will take you and your business to the promised land. Emotion. Uniqueness. Trust. Loyalty. Evangelism. These are the ingredients of the sustainable success I call *branding*.

First and foremost, please understand that this is not a specialized book for certain people within specific departments in a corporation. This book is for *every person* and *every department* within *any* industry—profit, nonprofit, big, small, social, or political. In short, this book is for everyone. Why? First, because *every company and every person is a brand*. You're a brand, your spouse is a brand, and so is your best friend, your neighbor, the public megacorporation and the little corner store—you get the idea! Moreover, this book is for everyone because it's about a *new* concept of branding that applies to businesses, organizations, and individuals alike.

Only you can develop your brand identity in a way that creates lasting, meaningful, and beneficial relationships. There is no doubt you are a brand. The question is, What is your brand right now and what do you want it to be? If you take the time with me to look at this new concept of what branding is, you'll be on your way to personal and professional success.

The ideas in this book are, collectively, a unique departure from the traditional understanding of brand creation, building, and maintenance. I developed my thinking on branding, and what makes a successful business, over more than 20 years of owning and running a national advertising agency, consulting with clients in a wide range of industries, and in more recent years on my work as an in-demand corporate speaker and trainer. I believe the way most people think about branding is stereotypical, tired, and narrow because it excludes the single most important feature of any human endeavor: sincere interaction with others. The branding I describe in this book is much larger than what the general understanding of the concept involves. It asks you to return to the moral principles that are at the heart of all sincere interaction. These principles are exemplified by some of our favorite children's stories, and so it is through these that I introduce you to each chapter and to a paradigm shift in thinking about branding.

The branding concept you learn about in the following chapters is divided into several elements. You learn what a brand is, how it is distinct from both advertising and marketing, who the loyal customer is, and how that customer is created through the ultimate customer experience. You also learn how to objectively assess just how good your organization is, right now, at creating the ultimate customer experience, and how you need to change to get to the level where you want to be. These ideas are relevant not only for the large companies mentioned in the pages of this book. Branding operates at the small company and personal levels, too. In fact, you see that a brand is about one's core identity; it's about the beliefs and values that make you the sort of person who always seeks to establish lasting, trusting relationships.

With the simple, direct processes you read about in this book, you will learn what *your* personal and professional brand could be. The same concepts apply in the virtual domain as well: E-mail and instant messaging, web pages and web-based companies, and other virtual platforms are also realms in which, increasingly, business is conducted, but this does not preclude them from the branding strategy I lay out in this book. In fact, my theory and practice of branding is crucial to the long-term success of any business that relies on technology. Once you understand branding in all its aspects, you'll see how your brand can be reconnected with advertising for an authentic fusion.

Get ready to rethink what you thought you knew about branding!

CHAPTER 1

YOU'RE NOT A MARKETING ANIMAL? THIS BOOK'S STILL FOR YOU!

Branding versus Advertising and Marketing—Completely Different Animals

THE STORY OF THE EAGLE, THE CROW, AND THE SHEPHERD

One warm afternoon, a crow sat on a tree branch enjoying the sights. He saw an eagle soaring high in the sky. I could do that, the crow thought to himself. I'm just as good at flying.

The crow continued to watch as the eagle swooped down on a lamb and grabbed it with its talons. As the eagle carried its dinner off into the air, the crow said, "I can do that!" So he took off from his branch and soared into the air, copying the pattern he had seen the eagle make. Then, when the crow saw a lamb stray from the flock, he dove down, alighting upon it just as he'd seen the eagle do. Of course, since he wasn't strong enough to lift both himself and the lamb off the ground, he couldn't very well fly away with it. But, just as he had grabbed hold, his claws had gotten stuck in the thick wool. The more he flapped his wings to extricate himself, the more entangled he became.

After first trying to run away from the unwelcome visitor on its back, the puzzled lamb eventually got used to the crow's presence and went back to browsing with the flock. Later that day, the shepherd found the crow. "What a strange thing for you to do," the shepherd said, untangling the bird as he held it fast. "Did you think you could steal my little lamb away?" Chuckling to himself, he put a string around the crow's leg and then took it home to his children for a pet.

The moral of the story: Advertising, marketing, and branding are not the same animals, nor can they accomplish the same thing!

YOU BUILD AND SUSTAIN THE BRAND!

Whether you work in management, accounting, manufacturing, customer service, sales, marketing, or any other department in an organization, you need to understand how branding differs from marketing and advertising. That's because, regardless of what your job is, *you*—not marketing and not advertising—build and sustain the brand. Once you understand how branding is a different animal from marketing and advertising, you'll understand why this book is for you. You'll see how important it is for you to be concerned about your company's brand, and what your role is in creating and sustaining it.

Suppose you work in manufacturing, and your job is to sit at a station and assemble a product. Because you have absolutely no contact with customers and you're not involved in marketing, you might think that your work has nothing to do with your employer's brand. Therefore, you might mistakenly think this book isn't for you. But consider the following scenario: Imagine that the product you manufacture has a flaw in it. It goes to the store, and the salesperson, who doesn't know about the flaw, is busy selling it. She's advocating on behalf of the product, which people know about because of the company's wonderful advertising. From advertising to sales pitch, the brand promise has been made. What happens to the brand when the customer learns about the flaw? It tanks. You, as part of the manufacturing and brand building process, fell short. Because of this, in the mind of the customer, the advertising was false and the salesperson was dishonest. The brand is damaged.

Or suppose you work in accounting. You might also conclude that this book isn't for you. After all, you're "internal." As such, you think you have nothing to do with the brand building process. But this is another mistaken conclusion. Imagine this scenario: A vendor calls asking for clarification on an invoice. You happen to be very busy that day. Because you don't consider your role as important to the brand building process, you treat the call as an intrusion, as insignificant. In the mind of the vendor, however, you represent your company and you are the brand. He tells friends and colleagues about his negative experience with your company. You've just damaged your company's brand. This book will show you that whatever it is you do, you impact your brand. So, it's crucial that you learn about my new brand paradigm.

Professionals and laypersons alike often don't properly distinguish between advertising, marketing, and branding. They think they are synonymous terms for a single function. The result, ultimately, is misapplication: People think they develop brands through advertising, or that their brand is simply the product or service for sale in the marketplace. This chapter is designed to dispel these mistaken ideas by defining what advertising, marketing, and branding are, and by clarifying their relationships to one another. By the end of this chapter, you'll have a working knowledge of each of these three concepts, both in their common usage and as I believe they should be understood. In Chapter 2, I focus exclusively on defining the concept of branding in a way that has not previously been articulated.

ADVERTISING AS AWARENESS

Most people focus on advertising as the single most important feature of both branding and marketing. It's understandable to think that advertising is the most important feature of a business' brand, given the fact that most of us are bombarded with advertising. A good ad makes consumers aware of a product or service, but it also makes the item attractive in order to compel them to seek it out. Advertisers have gone so far as to promote the idea that the product or service is so iconic that it *generates* a culture—Coca-Cola's "Coke is it"; Nike's "Just do it"—to which the consumer should want to belong. But at the end of the day, the function of advertising is simply to create brand *awareness* and hopefully drive customers to your place of business. No matter how flashy, savvy, sophisticated, or manipulative an advertisement is, the best it can do is make consumers aware of a product or service and possibly move them to investigate or even make a purchase. Convincing a customer to make a purchase, however, doesn't mean you've created a brand. What it does do is give you an *opportunity* to create and build a brand.

MARKETING AS A SYSTEM OF UNITING BUSINESSES AND CUSTOMERS

Advertising is one of the activities involved in marketing. So, what's marketing? Broadly speaking, it refers to those activities involved in the marketplace concerned with bringing products and services to consumers (and vice versa). The American Marketing Association defines marketing as "an organizational function and a set of processes for creating, communicating, and delivering value to customers and for managing customer relationships in ways that benefit the organization and its stakeholders." Marketing involves, among other things, research for gathering and analyzing data about customer demographics, customer perceptions, market size, strategies for developing and positioning a brand in the marketplace, the channel of distribution arrangement and management, and management of the sales force. In brief, marketing is a sort of social institution, a systematic way of bringing customers and businesses together to facilitate a sale. Initially, the marketplace was the physical location where goods and services were sold, and marketing derives its identity and basic methods from this original idea.

Notice that both advertising and marketing are mechanisms. As such, they are means of simply connecting customers and businesses. They are not brand experiences.

BRANDING IS A PROCESS OF CREATING AUTHENTICALLY UNIQUE, EMOTIONAL EXPERIENCES THAT YIELD EVANGELICALS

The common—and incorrect—understanding of branding in the world of marketing and advertising is a method of advertising to create and reinforce particular ideas of a product or service. Most people think a brand is a company's logo, image, or tagline—an identifying mark that differentiates one business from another in markets cluttered with similar products and services. Others think in terms of objects, namely, that a brand is a type of product manufactured by a company. In truth, branding is the creation and support of a powerful perception and image of someone or something based on unique, emotional experiences—so powerful that the perception or image becomes a belief. Therefore, I argue that the formula for professional and personal success lies in our ability to create the most powerful, emotional, memorable brand based on these unique experiences. As a result, branding operates at a level that is far more profound than is commonly thought.

Branding, as I conceive it, is a feeling. You *feel* trust, loyalty, comfort, love, need, desire, and happiness for brands because of beliefs derived from very precise experiences. What establishes this connection, however, has little to do with a product or a service. Some people initially get excited about the product or service because their introduction to it creates an expectation. But, just as advertising simply makes you aware of a product or service and marketing directs that awareness, buying a product or service only provides you with something you expect to

10

have. The *real* connection is established through person-to-person experience. What people get truly emotional about is the *process*, the experience of getting the thing—whatever it is—not the thing itself. The purchase is just the beginning, and only a small part of the brand building process. Advertising is a factor, but not the only one. After all, you can lead a horse to water, but you can't make him drink. In addition, although whatever you buy is useful and hopefully enjoyable, it's not what gives us the emotional experience that ultimately builds brand loyalty. Loyalty is expressed by what people say and do. Brand loyalty is expressed by what I call brand evangelism. In fact, brand loyalty is *critical* for brand evangelism.

Loyalty is created by human interaction, not objects. So the paradigm of powerful, emotional, positive brand building that I articulate enters the picture when *people* interact with each other in such a way that lasting emotional connections are made. Customers become evangelists, they become raving fans, because they trust the brand and they are loyal to it. In short, the brand is now part of their belief system because of the unique interpersonal experiences they have with that brand.

The facets of the unique experience are discussed at length in subsequent chapters, but at the outset, let me make one thing clear: Branding, as I conceive it, is not a gimmick; it's not manipulation. People who develop lasting brands know that in creating unique, emotional experiences one must be sincere. You won't be successful if people don't believe you're sincere; it's not about manipulating people to buy a product or service. It's creating a genuine experience and developing an authentic relationship between you and another person. Think about it this way: There are a few thoughts in the back of everyone's mind, thoughts we all share. We think about making more money, providing better for our family, spending more time with our family, doing better so we can contribute more to society, and perhaps most importantly, we think about how we can become better, more productive individuals. So, when you're sitting across from a customer, don't think about how much money they have and what they're buying. After all, the product is simply an offshoot of the better life they want. Instead, recall that they're thinking the same things you are. Get into the mind and soul of your customer and find out how to provide for them the things they would really love. Discover what would transform the moment and transform their lives, and do so in a genuine, sincere manner.

People outside the marketing and advertising professions typically think of a brand as a type of product manufactured by a particular company, be it a shoe, car, computer, hamburger, or some other object. At the same time, they also have strong emotional connections with particular brands. As a result, people then think that whatever feelings they have about the brand are really just about the object. But a brand is not simply a company's product, and the feelings we have about brands have little to do with the object in question. Take, for example, a can of soda. It's not simply *soda*, it's Coke or Pepsi or 7-Up. It's more than likely that you have some thoughts and feelings associated with at least one of these names. But this is just the *beginning* of the brand building process. Coca-Cola's advertisements try to trade on this idea. For years, television commercials have situated Coke in the context of people having certain emotional experiences. For example, in their "Hilltop" ad from 1971, young people sing "I'd like to teach the world to sing"

12

and replace one line with "I'd like to buy the world a Coke." Fast-forward to 2006, and Coca-Cola's "What Goes Around, Comes Around" television spot, which features people being nice to each other as we hear the lyrics "It's the right thing to do."

Now, none of this has to do with the taste or ingredients of the soft drink. It has to do with feelings we are meant to associate with the drink. These thoughts and feelings are based on specific *experiences*, and it is those experiences that largely determine your perception of a brand, both in the moment and collectively over time. If a company can give you the right experiences, they've been successful in developing their brand. Now let's take the related loyalty and branding concepts further. The fact is, I may like Coca-Cola but will buy it at one store and not another because of my experience with that store. Moreover, I'm only conditionally loyal to the drink itself. In a pinch, I may be perfectly happy drinking Pepsi. Loyalty does not run deep with an object. As I mentioned already, loyalty is an emotion and disposition people feel toward other people. When we do talk about object loyalty, we're only transferring loyalty we feel for people, and we do it in a limited way. A brand in the true sense of the concept is not limited to a product. It's also an experience; it's something you can't touch or see, but you can experience, such as insurance, air travel, dining out, cable television, and so on.

More often than not, we associate entire companies with brands, not just particular products. So we think of Apple, IBM, BMW, Ikea, Target, and hundreds of other large companies as brands. But these are not the only brands out there. There are hospitals and private schools, too. Medium-sized businesses, and even small mom-and-pop stores like the local hot dog stand are also brands.

Profit making companies are not the only organizations we associate with brands. Numerous charitable organizations, from the Red Cross and the Salvation Army to the Leukemia and Lymphoma Society and the Children's Miracle Network, are also brands. There is also the increasingly well-known Gates Foundation established by Microsoft founder and billionaire Bill Gates and Melinda Gates. Bill Gates carries on an American tradition of philanthropy begun by the descendants of tycoons like Andrew Carnegie, Henry and Edsel Ford, and John D. Rockefeller. There are charitable organizations devoted to symphonies, museums, and other arts; there are alumni associations and numerous important causes for which there are many nonprofit organizations. These are but a few charitable organizations that exist—all worthy of our patronage. So how do these groups distinguish themselves and successfully compete against one another? By creating unique brands that *over*deliver on the promises they make and by creating emotional, unique, and meaningful experiences for their customers and prospects.

I've sat on the boards of a number of charitable organizations focused on pediatric cancers. What got me connected was experiencing firsthand what these particular charities did. I became involved with the Center for Children's Cancer and Blood Disorders at University Hospital in Syracuse, New York, when I owned my own advertising agency. One of my clients was a big utility company, and one of its directors asked me for a favor. His son was being treated for a brain tumor at the center. Would I make up some brochures for a black-tie fund-raising auction coming up? Naturally, I said yes. He was a client, after all, and I went into the project thinking mildly that it was a nice extension of that relationship, but not much more. So I proceeded to get started on the brochures. However, it wasn't long before my company and I dove headfirst into the process, producing a video, a brochure, a new logo for the auction, and a title that lasts to this day, Little Gifts for Life.

What changed my involvement started with a phone call from the head oncologist at the center. He asked me to come up and take a tour of the center so I'd have a better understanding of what their work was all about. I agreed, and spent two hours walking the three floors the center occupies. I went from room to room where sick children were undergoing treatment or in the process of dying; I saw the equipment and medicines used; I saw rooms devoted to recreation for the kids who had the strength to get out of bed and play with toys, and lounge areas for parents to sit down, sip some coffee, and maybe have a moment or two of companionship with other parents. It was a devastating, transformative experience. On two occasions during the tour, I literally felt weak at the knees, and had to pause before continuing.

After I shook the doctor's hand and got on the elevator to leave, I realized I wasn't breathing—I couldn't breathe. I was having a visceral response to seeing small children undergoing brutal treatments and procedures like chemotherapy and surgeries. I couldn't get out of the hospital fast enough, practically gasping for air when I escaped through the front door. Completely overwhelmed, I crossed the street to the parking garage in tears. I sat in my car in complete confusion. This isn't right, I thought. Children are supposed to be healthy and have fun.

Parents are supposed to watch their children grow, not die. Why do these people suffer so much, while I am privileged to have four healthy, happy children?

Filled with thankfulness for my four healthy children, I was deeply affected by the terrible suffering these other children endured, but also how valiantly they fought to live, and what strong support their families gave them. Right then and there, I knew I would get involved and promote this charity's brand. I could not go through life without giving back. Because I was confronted with a unique brand and through a one-of-a-kind life-altering experience, I became a committed and longstanding evangelist to the cause.

WIDENING THE SCOPE OF WHAT CONSTITUTES A BRAND

Political and government institutions are brands, as are particular theories and schools of thought. For example, think about how the President of the United States develops and advances a particular brand. By means of domestic and international policy, the way in which the White House press secretary delivers the official governmental message, and other mechanisms, the United States becomes a brand. Some people think the brand promise is fulfilled, and others do not. It should come as no surprise that President George W. Bush's White House hired a Madison Avenue brand manager as undersecretary of state for Public Diplomacy and Public Affairs.

FEMA, the Federal Emergency Management Agency, was a little-known and poorly managed response agency before the mid-1990s. At that time, it underwent a dramatic overhaul, and its performance during and after a number of natural disasters bolstered its image. After the terrible events surrounding hurricane Katrina in 2005, the agency endured withering criticism and a blow to its brand identity.

The individuals who participate in politics are also brands. There are few among us who do not have strong views on politicians, and these views are based on the perception of those politicians' individual brands. The brand is not simply party affiliation, although both major parties in the United States are brands. For example, former Vice President Al Gore left political life in 2000 and retooled his brand. For a while he withdrew from political life, spending time as a visiting journalism professor at Columbia University's Graduate School of Journalism and continuing his work on global warming issues. With his speaking tour and the accompanying film *An Inconvenient Truth,* released in 2006, Gore emerged as a new and, some say, improved version of his brand.

As president, Bill Clinton's brand was so unique that he overcame several scandals and remained a wildly popular leader. While running for president in 1992, Clinton was dogged by stories about extramarital affairs. During his presidency, these stories persisted, leading to his impeachment by the House of Representatives. In addition, his and his wife's financial dealings in an investment known as Whitewater were investigated for years during his presidency. So unique and powerful was Clinton's brand, however, he was able to maintain excellent ratings as president despite the drama. A wealthy businessman who donates money to Clinton's philanthropic organization said in a 2006 *New Yorker* piece, "He's a brand, a world-wide brand, and he can do things and ask for things that no one else can."

You're Not a Marketing Animal?

An important component of Clinton's brand is that he has the ability to give to the people he meets personally his undivided attention, and this extends to his interactions with crowds, as well. He's a Rhodes scholar, has practically encyclopedic knowledge, is a political guru, and is a larger-than-life figure, but he also gives his full attention to whomever he's with, and this makes him human in a way he wouldn't be otherwise. For example, I had the honor and privilege to have dinner one evening with him and his wife, Senator Hillary Rodham Clinton, and another couple. It can be intimidating to speak with two powerful and important public figures whose lives are constantly bombarded by the needs and demands of millions of people. Still, the atmosphere they created at that dinner was one of intimacy and conviviality. Mr. and Mrs. Clinton not only knew my children's names, but also seemed to think it was genuinely important to know them as part of connecting directly with my wife and me.

President George W. Bush is also known for his personal touch. Everyone from members of his cabinet to journalists covering the White House beat is known according to a nickname chosen by Mr. Bush himself. But his brand is entirely different from Clinton's. Whereas Clinton is the poor kid from Arkansas who made good and, as president, reveled in the Washington political machinery, Bush is the wealthy kid from a political dynasty who is just a regular guy, a Texan who would rather be on his Crawford ranch clearing brush than at a black-tie affair in D.C. When running for president in 2000, Bush positioned himself as a guy's guy. He did not highlight his wealth or degrees from Yale and Harvard Business School. He distanced himself from questions about his Vietnam era National

Guard service, as well as business failings such as his stewardship of oil companies Arbusto and Harken Energy. In addition, just as Clinton was able to win the presidency despite stories about his infidelities, Bush was able to effectively circumvent stories about former drunk driving charges and drug use. What emerged instead was a regular guy who wanted to "restore integrity to the White House." Once averse to what he called nation building, the post–September 11 president redefined much of his brand to win reelection as a wartime president determined to secure the safety of the American people he was sworn to protect.

Internationally, Clinton and Bush are known as very different brands. Beloved by the majority of Western countries and quite a few in the Far East, Clinton enjoys a reputation as a consensus builder. Bush, in contrast, is known more as a maverick, someone who demands that others recognize the rightness of his position. As such, he's alienated many. In both cases, the men inhabiting the Oval Office developed their own brands.

Consider your favorite celebrity—a movie star, singer, or other entertainer—and you once again are thinking about a brand. Oprah Winfrey is one such individual who has cultivated a remarkably successful brand over the past 20-plus years. Though best known as a talk show host, Ms. Winfrey is also a film producer, actor, magazine publisher, and philanthropist. In fact, her brand transcends all her endeavors, because her brand is that of a genuine, trustworthy, honest, caring, hardworking, intelligent, no-nonsense, and successful woman. When Oprah started her book club, little-known titles suddenly shot to the top of best-seller lists simply because people trusted Oprah's brand. Oprah *is* her brand! Though most people have likely never met her, they feel connected to her.

This connection is set in stark relief when it's severed in some significant way. The point of calling out the following individuals is to prove that no matter how powerful or wonderful a brand is—personally or professionally—that brand can be quickly and forever damaged when negative activities occur. Let's take three examples from recent memory: Kenneth Lay, Tom Cruise, and Mel Gibson. The late Ken Lay, former CEO of the failed energy company Enron, was not a household name before Lay and Enron colleagues were indicted on various criminal charges in connection with Enron's collapse. In almost no time at all, Enron went from being the darling of the energy world, with Lay its hero, to being the company that bilked shareholders and employees alike out of millions of dollars. Many employees lost their entire 401(k) savings. Lay was faced with 11 criminal charges, including securities fraud and insider trading charges. He was later convicted of securities fraud and conspiracy, but died before he was sentenced. His actions negatively impacted many people, and before he died, his name—his brand—looked to be irrevocably tarnished.

Two megawatt movie stars have also found that their actions have undermined their brand. Tom Cruise and Mel Gibson have been wildly successful movie stars for years, and they built successful businesses because they had popular brands. Both were known to bring audiences into theaters, thereby generating billions of dollars in ticket sales and merchandising opportunities. What brought audiences into the theaters was their brand promise. Moviegoers knew what they were getting when they went to see a Mel Gibson or Tom Cruise movie, specifically the Cruise or Gibson brand of action or dramatic hero. Unfortunately, each star's actions have received negative press, which has tarnished their brands. In other words, their actions were not consistent with their brands.

In 2005, Tom Cruise made very public and repeated proclamations of his love for the actress Katie Holmes, and people found his behavior peculiar. At the same time, Cruise became increasingly vocal about his Scientology-based views on psychiatry and the use of antidepressants and other psychiatric drugs. His behavior struck many as not only odd, but also wrongheaded and inappropriate. Although it's not entirely possible to tell whether the lukewarm box office receipts for his latest release, *Mission Impossible: III*, are due to the public's turning away from his brand because of his actions, the fact that Paramount Studios severed its long-standing ties with Cruise's production company is telling. It was widely reported in various media outlets from CNN to *Daily Variety* that Sumner Redstone, the CEO of Viacom, Paramount's parent company, claimed that Cruise's behavior cost the studio over $150 million.

Gibson's personal life also has damaged his brand. In the summer of 2006, Gibson was arrested near his Malibu, California, home on a charge of driving under the influence (DUI). That by itself would not destroy his brand, but what he did at the time of his arrest has unquestionably harmed the formerly well-respected, Oscar-winning actor and director. Anti-Semitic statements uttered during a tirade shocked and outraged many people. Though some believe the statements do not reflect Gibson's true feelings because they were made while he was intoxicated, many remain appalled. In an interview with Diane

Sawyer in October 2006 on *Good Morning America*, Gibson came off to many as insincere. Part of the problem is what he said: "What I need to do is to heal myself and to be assuring and allay the fears of others and to heal them if they had any heart wounds from something I may have said." He did not take responsibility for his anti-Semitic remarks. Instead, "if" people were hurt by what he "may have said," he's sorry. To many, he seemed more interested in blaming his words and actions on alcohol, calling them "just the stupid rambling of a drunkard."

If a celebrity is known for their brand—action hero, dramatic artist, family-friendly films—what happens when that celebrity fails to live up to it? The brand is the individual's calling card, the seal of approval, the *character* everyone is supposed to count on. That character extends to making amends for wrongdoings. In Gibson's case, that would have involved owning up to what he said as part of who he was. At that point, he could have said, "Look, I don't like that about myself. I want to change it." Taking responsibility for oneself is crucial to winning back the trust lost over incidents such as Gibson's anti-Semitic statements. Without truly taking responsibility for what he said, his brand power is diluted.

I'M A BRAND, YOU'RE A BRAND—WE'RE ALL BRANDS!

Brands are not limited to inanimate objects, institutions, and internationally known public figures. Any individual is a brand. Think about the last time you found yourself sitting around talking with people about someone you all know. You most likely talked about that individual's personality and character, or told stories about experiences you've had with that person that shaped your view of who that individual is. This, too, means that the individual is a brand. Whether you're thinking about *your* dry cleaner, *your* coffee shop, *your* market, you're thinking about a brand you've grown to trust and to which you are loyal. That's why each place is "yours." In fact, you are a brand yourself, as are your kids, your friends, and your neighbors. I'm a brand, too. Each of us is a brand, which means each of us deeply affects those around us. On a daily basis, each of us transforms moments for others—hopefully always to the better, but sometimes not. That's why it's important to understand what it means to be a brand and to understand your own brand.

One of the first things I do when starting a corporate presentation is demonstrate my brand. To distinguish myself from a myriad of other speakers, I have to place my brand on my audience. When I've finished, they have the Scott Deming brand all over them. It's like being tattooed—except it's actually fun instead of painful! I do it with a mind reading effect. I call someone from the audience up onstage. I then turn to the audience and ask them, "What is the one thing, no matter what we do, that we have to deal with day after day? That one thing is numbers—numbers of all sorts, from payroll, to sales goals, to quarterly profits, to withholding taxes. You name it, numbers are involved. Today, we're going to deal with a very specific number." Then I turn to the individual I've brought onstage, and I say, "We're here to help you grow your business. Therefore, I'd like you to concentrate on a sales goal. I don't want this to be a sales goal that can be accomplished at the drop of a hat. So, think of something lofty, something unattainable. But for demonstration purposes, your goal must be represented by a two-digit number. Got it? Okay, don't tell me what it is; just concentrate on it."

At this point, I draw a grid on a large piece of paper and fill in each section with a different number—sort of like a checkerboard filled with distinct numbers. After the grid is completed, I ask the audience member if her number is written anywhere on the board. "No, I don't see it," she says. I turn to the audience and say, "She's focusing on a lofty, unattainable number. You know when you want to accomplish something lofty, you can't do it on your own. You need help from many different resources. You also can't approach it from a single direction. You have to approach it from many directions. That's what I'm going to help you do here today."

In about 10 seconds, I add the numbers in every direction—rows, columns, diagonally, four in the corner, four in the middle. As I add, I say, "No matter how impossible it seems, if you step out of your box and approach things from a different perspective, you can achieve the impossible." Turning to my audience participant, I ask, "Does your number appear now?" With an astonished nod, she affirms that every four-box total in every possible direction adds up to her thought-of goal.

The point of all this is to show the audience how to transform the moment. After that, I've got them hooked for the next hour. When the demonstration is finished, and the oohs and ahhs and applause have quieted down, I ask a simple question: "Based on what you just experienced, how would you categorize me as a speaker? Would you say I'm a typical speaker or would you say I am a unique and different speaker?" Everyone shouts, "Unique!" "Different!" "Right," I tell them. "In less than five minutes I was able to create a vivid and lasting impression in your minds of who I am and what type of speaker I am. You see, in the sea of speakers—literally thousands of speakers all vying for your business—I must be unique if I'm going to successfully compete. Now, you all knew you were going to get a speaker. You read about me and heard about me. But you did not, could not truly understand beforehand the type of speaker I would be. You could not fully know my my brand of speaking until now. And now that I've delivered something completely unexpected, emotional, and unique, you understand my brand. I'm hoping by the time I'm done, you'll be so impacted and so impressed that if anyone ever asks you if you know of a good speaker, you'll say, 'Do I ever! His name is Scott Deming. He's not just a speaker—he's a great speaker, a unique speaker, a speaker with a twist!'"

I'm not trying to peddle my speaking services here, in this book. However, I am trying to make a very important point about a very misunderstood topic called Branding. Based on their experiences with me, audience members associate me, as a brand, with thoughts and feelings of positive uniqueness. Rather than walking onstage and standing at a lectern to give a speech, I engage the audience in a way that is completely unique among corporate speakers. That not only differentiates me from other speakers, it also creates an experience in the audience not soon forgotten—and one that audience members want to share with others.

I've just briefly explained my own brand as a way to help you understand the importance of making a unique, unexpected emotional connection to your customer. Each of us is unique, as is each business, organization, and institution. That means that there is no standard answer for what makes any given brand experience unique. The sort of individual interaction that's involved in a unique experience is not mechanistic. Each of us perceives our experiences in different ways; our emotional triggers are not all the same. Therefore, it is crucial that you treat the brand building process as a process of creating *individual* relationships.

As we have seen, marketing and its advertising arm have very little to do with relationships of the sort crucial to branding. In this chapter, we've discovered that there's a big difference between creating a message, structuring a marketing program, and creating a brand.

In the pages and chapters to follow, we will see a paradigm shift from the old branding concepts to the one I'm articulating. Be prepared, because this isn't your father's branding book!

CHAPTER 2

THIS IS NOT YOUR FATHER'S BRANDING FORMULA

Defining a Brand

"THE TORTOISE AND THE HARE"

Once upon a time there was a very arrogant hare. "I can run faster than anyone!" he boasted to every forest animal he saw. He especially loved to tease the tortoise, who everyone agreed was faster only than the snail, and not by much at that. Hopping back and forth over the tortoise's back, the hare would squeal with glee. "I can run faster than you can!"

Finally, the tortoise had had just about all he could take of the furry braggadocio. "Just who do you think you are?" demanded the tortoise. "No one denies you are swift; anyone can see that. But even you can be beaten!"

The hare fell to the ground, emitting peals of laughter as his fluffy white tail and large hind feet wiggled in the air. When he had finally recovered his composure, the hare sprang back on his legs and looked at the tortoise. "Me, beaten in a race?" He tried to stifle a laugh but couldn't help giggling. "By whom, *you*? Surely not you, or anybody else, for that matter. Nobody in the world can win a race against me. I'm just too speedy."

The tortoise slowly blinked at the hare. Then he said, "Yes, me. I can win a race against you."

The hare burst into laughter again, and said, "Okay, then, why don't you try?"

Word spread across the forest quickly, and all the animals gathered together to plan a course for the race. At dawn the next day, the tortoise and hare stood at the starting line. Yawning, the hare said to the tortoise, "How about I give you a head start? I could use a little more sleep, anyway."

With the whistle's shrill cry, the forest creatures cheered the start of the race. As the tortoise started slowly off down the path, the hare called after him, "Take your time! I'll have my 40 winks and catch up with you in a minute."

After a fitful sleep, the hare awoke. Looking around, he saw that the tortoise had not made much headway on the course. "Well, then," he said stretching. "I could have a little breakfast, too." Eyeing some cabbages in a nearby field, the hare hopped off to have something to eat.

His stomach full and the late morning sun warming his fur, the hare began to get sleepy. "I could just have a little nap before I dash to the finish line and handily win the race. Besides," he said, gazing at the tortoise's slow progress, "it will take but a minute to catch up." So the hare fell asleep with a smile on his face, envisioning the look of surprise on the tortoise's face as the hare blew by.

At the end of the day, as the sun slowly set in the western hills, the tortoise was finally a yard from the finish line. The hooting and hollering of the forest creatures woke the hare from a deep, snoring slumber.

Catching a glimpse of the tortoise in the distance, the hare took off after him. Dashing along the course, the hare leapt and bounded after the tortoise, who was only a small dark dot on the horizon. Soon the hare's tongue was hanging out, and every breath was a great gasp for air, but he was now fast approaching the tortoise. With just one more leap, he would overtake his challenger and win the race. But the hare's last leap was one leap too late, for at that very moment, the tortoise had crossed over the finish line and had beaten the hare!

Exhausted and humiliated, the hare slumped in disgrace against a nearby tree. The tortoise looked over at him, and a slow smile spread across his face. "Slow and steady wins the race every time."

The moral of the story: Be careful what you promise. When you make a promise, you create expectations. When you exceed expectations, you create a brand.

SUCCESSFUL BRANDS DEFY EXPECTATIONS

I'll bet the forest animals were talking for weeks afterward about the tortoise's amazing performance and how the hare had finally been knocked down a peg! Both characters have something to teach us. First, the hare lost the race not because he wasn't really the fastest of the forest runners, but because he had rested on his laurels. Everyone expected him to win—just as he had promised—and not only did he not fulfill those expectations, he disappointed the crowd terribly. He didn't just fail to deliver on his promise, he failed *miserably*. Moreover, his overinflated ego was his ultimate downfall. In Chapter 6 I talk more about the dangers of overestimating your brand, but for the moment, let's focus on what the tortoise accomplished.

The tortoise defied expectations. He gave the forest animals an experience they wouldn't soon forget, and in doing so, he altered their perception of what sort of character he was. He was now held in the highest regard. He was popular and exceptional. Everyone wanted to be with him and everyone evangelized about him. That's what brand building is all about: creating unique, memorable, and emotional experiences that create customer loyalty.

Recall from Chapter 1 that a brand is a dynamic concept. It involves deeply personal, emotional connections established by unique experiences that transcend the ordinary. When branding is successful, something important and meaningful happens. More often than not, however, brands fail because the individual or company does not have the appropriate attitude and approach toward building and sustaining the brand.

When individuals and companies don't deliver on their brand promise, they fail like the hare in the story you just read and the young shepherd in "The Boy Who Cried 'Wolf.'" I call these companies Wolf Brands, like the title story you read in the Introduction, because they make proclamations and promises that fall flat. In so doing, they fail to unite the two aspects of their brand just described. Not only do they not deliver on their brand promise, they fail to create or maintain uniqueness in their brand category. At one time or another, numerous companies have failed to deliver: New Coke, pets.com, Sears,

Carrier, Hewlett-Packard, General Motors, Ford, Nike, Exxon, Wendy's, Capital One, Sony, Wal-Mart, Enron—the list goes on and on.

Sears, for example, was at one time the preeminent department store. There wasn't a product they didn't carry, and all of them were backed by a guarantee of quality. When you heard the name Sears, you knew you could count on what you got. And, if something didn't work the way it was supposed to or stopped working altogether, Sears was ready with a replacement or quality repair. Unfortunately, that time seems to have passed. My personal experience is a testament to the new Sears brand.

For 20 years, my wife and I had been loyal Sears customers. Then one day I got a pair of scissors and cut up our store cards.

"What are you doing?" my wife asked.

"I'm calling them on their failed promises," I responded.

"Good," she agreed, and she gave me her card as well.

In Chapter 7, I discuss the Sears story in detail, but for now the relevant point is that Sears failed miserably as a brand. Not only did it fail to deliver on its promise—the same promise it's made for decades—it also failed to exceed my expectations with a unique experience when I needed it most. The entire Sears brand, in my mind, failed because of a single experience I had with one young lady, a supposed customer service representative. She did everything in her power to do the minimum so she could get off the phone and go back to whatever she was doing. That experience soured me on Sears, and I no longer trust the Sears brand. More important, I also go around antievangelizing them at every opportunity. And believe me, this is not good for Sears. In my capacity as a corporate presenter, I have the opportunity to speak to lots of people!

On the other hand, there are companies that have worked extremely hard to overdeliver on their brand promises, and thereby have created positive brands, even if there have been missteps along the way: Apple, Dell, eBay, Whole Foods, BMW, Mercedes-Benz, Super 8 Motels, Verizon Wireless, Saturn, Harley Davidson, Disney, NASCAR, Anheuser-Busch, Microsoft, Starbucks, Google, Ben & Jerry's, Home Depot, Calvin Klein, Chuck E. Cheese—again, the list goes on and on. There are hundreds of thousands of small, medium, and large businesses across the globe. A successful brand is not simply one that represents a good product. The product merely gets you in the game. It's what the brand does that makes all the difference to sustained success.

Here's an example to illustrate my point. I had the opportunity to deliver a series of presentations to the executives, operations, sales, and marketing departments of Royal Caribbean Cruise Lines. It was their first international branding summit, and they held it on their brand new ship, *Freedom of the Seas*, the largest ship in the world, a week before its maiden voyage. Several hundred of us set sail from Boston en route to Miami. Over the course of four days members of the cruise line conducted themselves as if this was an ordinary public cruise. When there were no meetings or presentations in session, people could experience what a Royal Caribbean cruise was like. Crew members created experiences for the staff of Royal Caribbean as though they were guests. They were helpful and conciliatory; they put on parades down the Grande Promenade one evening, and set up Mojito and karaoke parties on the top deck near one of their many pools with live music and DJs. Three phenomenal meals—both in presentation and taste—

were served every day in the luxurious dining facilities by a most attentive staff. The practically Dionysian parties and generally festive atmosphere combined with the terrific attitude of the staff made the cruise experience unique.

It was fantastic, and I wanted to see even more of this remarkable ship. So when I had some down time, I went to look around the massive floating entertainment center. The size of the ship alone was impressive, like the size of a small city. But on top of that, the stores, restaurants, casino, and ballrooms were decorated with expensive chandeliers, marble floors, beautiful artwork, and baroque details. I should have been wowed by all its grandeur, but I wasn't. Why? Because they were all empty. A ship as large as the one we were on holds upwards of 3,000 passengers, and with only a fraction on board, the majority of the ship's amenities were unused.

I filed these observations away for the last of my four presentations. The first day was for senior management, while the second day saw back-to-back sales and marketing presentations. On the third day I addressed the entire organization in the ship's ice arena, typically used for ice shows. Parquet flooring covered the ice, and I had the entire stage for my talk, while the organization's members filled up the stadium style seating.

I talked about how products and services merely get you in the game and said that a successful brand is one that creates and sustains a specific perception based on unique, emotional experiences. "If you really want to understand what I mean by this, just once before this trip is over, walk around this extraordinary ship. That's what I did. After my presentations were over, while you were all in meetings, I spent a lot of time walking around, observing this incredible vessel. But you know what I noticed most? It was emotionless. Absolutely nothing on this ship without *people* involved could create any emotion. Until people get excited, the ship's not a brand. What happens on the ship is the brand," I told the assembly. "You've got gorgeous artwork, chandeliers, and marble floors, but all of that is not what people really come for. People come for memorable experiences—like the parade your staff put on. Stuff doesn't get people emotional, *people* do. You've got a remarkable ship, and it's outfitted beautifully, but this stuff could be found anywhere—I could be anywhere. I could be in a Vegas casino or an expensive hotel. You see, it's not just about how beautiful the ship is. The ship and all the beautiful stuff on it merely get you in the game. It's more about the hooting and hollering you hear in the casino when someone hits the jackpot, or the oohs and aahs of kids watching the parade, or the laughter of adults and kids alike as they're completely lost in utter enjoyment of your water park on the top deck. It's the emotional response everywhere, created not by your *stuff*, but by your *staff*. The experience is not just of the ship's beauty; it's also of the people. And it is *this* reason people get tied to the ship, and to the brand, and the two become one."

For weeks afterward, I got tremendous feedback from the cruise participants. The idea that *they* created the brand really hit home. If nothing else, I wanted the folks at Royal Caribbean to understand just what their brand is and how it works. If they tied their brand concept to their ships alone, instead of the experiences people had with one another on the ship, they'd eventually fail to deliver on their brand promise.

Each company that failed to deliver on its brand promise, or succeeded in delivering it, had certain expectations about what their brand was and what it did. Part of the branding process involves generating certain experiences for the customer that leave lasting impressions. Brands that succeed are those perceived by the customer in very specific ways. In the cases when a brand failed, the customer did not perceive the brand the way the company wanted her to. In Chapter 4, we focus specifically on customer experience, but for the moment, think about it this way: Experiences are *meaningful*. We give meaning to every experience we have. If we didn't, our lives would probably be much more like a cat's than a human being's: stimulus response. For example, when we experience a physical sensation, it has meaning; we're aware not just of the fact of a feeling, but the feeling's meaning as pain or pleasure, something to be avoided or pursued. We don't simply and unthinkingly recoil or move toward the object that causes the sensation. So part of the process of creating a brand is generating the "right" feelings in the customer. In this way, the customer will perceive the brand "correctly."

DEFYING EXPECTATIONS MEANS *OVERDELIVERING ON YOUR BRAND PROMISE*

A successful brand is one that unites the "right" feelings with the "correct" perceptions. These right feelings are generated by the customer experiencing not just what is expected, but by experiencing the *over*delivery on a promise made. But how does one come to expect anything to begin with? Expectations come not only from direct experience, but also from word of mouth, advertising claims, public relations, and more. Suppose, for example, you walk into your local Target. For any number of reasons, you expect to find things you need; after all, your perception of Target is a department store that sells everything from clothing to car seat covers. What Target must do is not simply deliver on the promise of having durable goods at reasonable prices. They have to create in the minds of the customer a perception about Target that is positively unique and unexpected. Thus, a successful brand will, at the very least match up with the customer's expectation. However, a *distinct* brand will blow away that expectation or create an entirely new one.

Starbucks has grown to optimize the idea of creating a brand by generating so-called correct perceptions. The Starbucks brand is not entirely about coffee. To reiterate, the product only gets them in the game. What makes the brand and keeps the customers coming back are the experiences and associations. The Starbucks brand is the reason we're willing to stand in line way too long and gladly pay way too much for a cup of coffee. We take our recyclable cup out of the store and into our workplace. We show, through our purchase, how sophisticated we are, how we know about the finer things in life. By associating with the Starbucks brand, we associate with success.

Another example of a successful brand is BMW. It's been around a while longer than Starbucks and sells an entirely different product, but the corporation's understanding and delivery of its brand is remarkably similar. When you think of The Ultimate Driving Machine, you don't think of a mere car; you think of how the car reflects your status in society, that you've "made it." You think of exceptional performance, reliability and safety, tradition, and craftsmanship. BMW created their brand through repeatedly exceptional experiences for their customers. From purchase to service, each member of the dealership's staff treats each customer like a celebrity. Though dealerships are individually owned, the corporate culture generates the brand, and the dealers execute it time and time again. Each team works together to create the ultimate buying experience.

Once you're in the car, you have the BMW driving experience. Through its performance, you can feel the price and status of this car. Nothing else hugs a turn or gets past an 18-wheeler quite like a BMW. And people notice you in your brand new Beemer, which is another element of the whole experience. It's an experience you love, and you find yourself wanting to share with others.

Luxury is not the only brand. Saturn, the little car company that could, established a family brand—a culture, if you will—of hassle-free sales, excellent service, and honest, down-to-earth transactions. Saturn doesn't make the most expensive or high performance car in the world, but it creates an experience many people want to have. Their stated "brand purpose," in fact, is "to surprise and delight people in all aspects of the auto motive experience." The Saturn brand survives because it delivers on its brand promise. It tells us it's "a different kind of car company," and it is. If a story mentioned in a 2005 *Business-Week Online* article by Diego Rodriguez is to be believed, Saturn really *is* a different kind of car company. Rodriguez writes, "Recently, a man called Saturn's customer-service number with a big problem: His daughter's car had broken down in Arizona, and she was stranded. He reported her location, her license plate number—and the fact that her car was a Honda. When the Saturn representative pointed this out to the upset father, he said, "You're the company that cares about people, and that's why I called you." What would your company do? Saturn sent out a truck to pick her up, towed her Honda, and let her father know that she was safe.

The reason Saturn succeeds is not because they make a better car than, say, Honda but because they *over*deliver on their brand promise. On top of that, when you go to buy a Saturn, you have a unique, hassle free, pressure free, worry free, and innovative buying experience. It's not the *car*, it's the car *company*. As Rodriguez rightly points out, "A brand is about what you do, or don't do, and not what you say." Clearly, Saturn is a "do" company.

Disney also delivers on its brand promise. We all know what the Disney logo means, and likely we all have had similar experiences at the famed Disney amusement parks. This is the place where all kids' dreams become reality, and all adults become kids, because every employee works to overdeliver on the Disney brand promise. It's the ultimate family vacation, the wholesome family movies, the feeling of wonderment, and the recognition of the iconic Magic Kingdom castle. "If you can dream it, you can make it happen." The magic of dreams is Disney's brand, and it's delivered by a journey that ends with the exuberant feeling that nothing is impossible. It's a simple brand concept, really. As Walt Disney himself said, "Remember, this all started with a mouse." Yet as simple as it is, the brand continues to inspire millions, young and old alike.

Where Disney's brand is the magic of dreams for kids and families, Harley Davidson's brand is the fantasy of being an outlaw. When asked what Harley sells, a top Harley executive said, "We sell a forty-three-year-old accountant the ability to dress in leather, drive down a street in a small town, and make everybody afraid of him!" Harley doesn't just sell motorcycles. It sells the association with a particular lifestyle, a brotherhood of out-laws. It's not about the bike—though it's a great bike—because it's not the only great one out there. Harley owners and Harley riders are not just riding a Harley bike; they're living the Harley life. And talk about brand evangelists, they've got the Harley logo everywhere: on their belts, boots, shirts, jackets, wallets, key rings, hats, and coffee mugs. I've heard some of these folks have the Harley logo tattooed on their butts. True! Once your logo's been tattooed on someone's rear end, you know you've made it.

To sum up, the core of a highly successful brand is its ability to create a feeling of belonging, of culture and family by overdelivering on its promise to its customers. It is this delivery that amounts to the ultimate customer experience. In turn, the ultimate customer experience creates just the sort of customer you want: one who brings you more business. Don't forget, it's the job of the brand to create value and need—"unique" is the operative word—so that customers' associations with a brand are visceral and durable. As a 1995 *Advertising Age* article asserts, "Branding, be it global or domestic, can be explained with the following metaphor: Long term brand loyalty is akin to getting the consumer to marry a brand, and requires that the marketer provide the same set of information one needs to decide upon marrying a person; information about the physical attributes, the style and character of the brand." Branding is about creating such an intense emotional connection that the customer feels married, feels a sense of belonging. When you marry someone, you expect that person to remain monogamous, and that's the same feeling you want someone to have about your brand.

CHAPTER 3

You Got What You Came For—I Did My Job . . . Didn't I?

A Typical Service versus a Unique Experience

"The Crow and the Pitcher"

There once were two thirsty crows sitting on a barren tree. Because there was a drought, all the rivers and ponds had dried up, and it had been days since the two crows had had even a drop of water. "Whatever will we do?" one crow asked the other. "I am so thirsty. I think my wings are drying out!" He spread his wings to reveal dull feathers, some of which fell off and floated to the dirt road below.

The other crow sighed. "I don't know what we'll do. I expect we will die of thirst."

Just then, a traveler passed by, stopped, and then turned around and sat beneath the tree. He pulled out a glass bottle and sack from his backpack, and began to eat his lunch. When he took a pull from his bottle, the crows looked on longingly. After a while, the traveler got up and walked on, leaving behind his bottle. "Look!" the first crow cried. "He's forgotten his pitcher. Let's go see what's inside. Maybe there's water, and we won't die of thirst after all!"

The two crows swooped down and investigated the bottle. First one and then the other stuck his beak inside, but the neck of the bottle was too long, and the liquid inside was too far down for the crows to reach. "Oh wretched day!" the second crow wailed. "There is water inside, and we are so close but cannot reach it. Surely we will die of thirst."

While the second crow bemoaned his fate and expected the worst, the first crow was busy thinking. Looking around, the first crow spied some pebbles in the dirt. One by one, he dropped pebbles into the glass bottle, and the water began to rise. Eventually, it reached the top of the neck. "Here is your water," the first crow said. "Take a long drink."

The second crow was overcome by his friend's ingenuity and the unexpected reversal of what seemed like an inevitable fate. After drinking enough to gain his strength, he stepped aside so his ingenious friend could partake of the water, too. When both were refreshed, they had the energy to fly away from the drought-ravaged land and find a place with plenty to eat and drink.

The moral of the story: Create the unexpected, transform the moment.

BUILDING A BRAND DOESN'T HAPPEN OVERNIGHT (DON'T KILL YOUR GOLDEN GOOSE!)

When Larry Page and Sergey Brin, the creators of the wildly popular Internet search engine Google, decided to take their company public in 2004, they did something unusual. In their public offering prospectus, they wrote an Introduction in which they outlined their ideas about what an investor should expect from Google. Acknowledging that traditional public companies keep their eyes on quarterly earnings to gauge their financial health, Page and Brin said they would eschew such practices. Why? Isn't a public company's responsibility to its shareholders preeminent? Isn't a public company's responsibility defined by how it repays its investors? The short answer, according to Page and Brin was no—at least not in the short term. They wrote, "A management team distracted by a series of short term targets is as pointless as a dieter stepping on a scale every half hour." In other words, anyone who wants to invest in Google has to be "on board" with Google's stated mission, and this mission did not include rewarding the "make a quick buck" investor.

Think about the classic fable "The Goose That Laid the Golden Egg." It's about a husband and wife who owned a special goose. Each morning, the couple would awaken to find the goose had laid for them a golden egg—solid gold, through and through. Delighted with their daily treasure, they soon became very rich.

Unfortunately, however, their riches did not content them. They wanted more and more and more, and they wanted it faster. Soon enough, the husband and wife began to gripe about the size of each egg, and the 23 hours in between each delivery. "Why must this goose wait so long before laying another egg?" the husband asked irritably. "I don't know," responded the wife. "But it *is* very inconvenient, isn't it?" After further consideration, the wife said, "It must be made of gold, mustn't it?" The husband replied, "Indeed it must." "Then," said the wife, "we could get more if we opened the goose right up." And so they crept up upon the goose as she lay sleeping in her nest of straw, and sliced her open with a knife. "Where is it?" yelled the wife in alarm. "Where is the gold?" "It must be here somewhere," answered the husband. "It must be."

But there was nothing in the goose but flesh and bone. Not even a fleck of gold was to be found. In their greed, the couple had ruined the only source of their wealth, and before long, the golden eggs they had collected were gone. The husband and wife died penniless.

There is no way to build or sustain a brand with a get rich quick mentality that ignores the value of the customer and the business. Google's Brin and Page were clearly aware of the pitfalls of a get rich quick mentality. You can attain success—your own golden egg, if you will—without killing the goose!

By releasing their unusual introduction to their public offering prospectus, Brin and Page were effectively interviewing prospective investors, not the other way around! They seemed to be saying, We know what we're all about, and if you agree with what we're doing and how we're doing it, you should join us. Your commitment will be rewarded not by short term gains, but long term, brand-building goals. Building a lasting brand is not the result of slipshod, fast-turnaround practices. In fact, such practices are how brands are destroyed. Brin and Page defined their investors, rather than being defined by them.

This chapter is not about public companies per se, but the Google example provides an entrée into a discussion about types of business models—really, types of thinking about how to relate to your customer. Specifically, this chapter is about the important distinction between transactions, typical services, and unique experiences. In fact, all three are not only types of experiences; they are also ways that businesses think about themselves and their customers. A transaction is simply an exchange of money for a good or service. A typical service is simply giving to the customer what he expects to get. A unique experience transcends the expected and becomes a one-of-a-kind, loyalty-building emotional relationship.

Whether your organization is a political party, a charitable organization, a small, privately owned company, a set of franchises, or a public megacorporation, understanding the distinction between a transaction, a service, and a unique experience is crucial to building a lasting brand. Though we discuss the two-sidedness of transactions, services, and unique experience—in other words, how they are reflected on both the side of the business and the customer—the emphasis in this chapter is on how you can understand the difference between transactional, typical service, and unique experience orientations in thinking. Once you understand what the difference is, we move on to discuss what you need to do to transcend transactional or typical service-oriented thinking. This brings us back to Google.

When businesses get mired in sales quotas, short-term goals, statistics, and so forth, the people inside those businesses become robotic. Their eyes are focused not on how the brand is doing, but on what the numbers tell them. In a sense, this is the result of a misunderstanding of a free-market economy. When the operating principle of competing successfully in the marketplace is made manifest in dollar signs, trouble follows. Does this mean people shouldn't try to make money, and lots of it?

Of course not! But making money is the *result* of a successful brand, not its driving mechanism. To paraphrase world-renowned writer, management consultant, and professor, Peter Drucker, "People on Wall Street think that we're in the business of making money. We're in the business of selling shoes. Making money is the *result* of selling shoes."

Brin and Page's 2004 letter to investors seems to reflect a deep understanding of this concept. If Google management's eyes are on quarterly earnings reports because it thinks serving the investor's immediate financial interests is paramount, several negative consequences will follow. First, the businesses' practices will all be oriented around what the numbers say. Numbers will dictate how each division, department, manager, and staff member does its job. As Brin and Page wrote, "The standard structure of public ownership may jeopardize the independence and focused objectivity that have been most important in Google's past success and that we consider most fundamental for its future." In other words, they're not going to follow the traditional numbers-based model.

Those companies that do, however, follow the numbers model bring about the second negative consequence. Companies that focus on numbers to the exclusion of everything else turn away from the practices that made the business worth taking public in the first place. The function of the business is thereby fundamentally altered. Third, since the attention is on the numbers that will keep investors happy, the customer effectively disappears. At best, the customer becomes a cog in the business' machinery of making money. That's the *last* thing any company should want their customer to be!

Consider your own business. Most likely, you sell products

or offer services that other businesses in your area also provide. In terms of your content, there's no difference between you and your competition. So there's no reason why a customer would choose to patronize your business rather than another one that's at a more convenient location. You must consider, then, what you can do to differentiate your business from all the others that offer the same services or products. The differentiator must be the level of service, the unique experience you offer each of your customers. You have to engender loyalty in customers so that they will go out of their way to shop with you, regardless of how far out of their way they have to go to get to you.

BUILDING A BRAND: A MERE TRANSACTION, A TYPICAL SERVICE, OR A UNIQUE EXPERIENCE?

Before focusing our discussion on the difference between a transaction, a typical service, and a unique experience, let's bring several concepts together. By doing so, we should be able to make clear the significance of focusing your business on unique experiences rather than on typical services or transactions. We know the basic distinction between advertising and branding, and marketing and branding is one of awareness. Advertising and marketing make customers aware of your product, goods, or service. Branding transcends that to become an emotional relationship between customer and brand. A brand establishes a relationship through emotional experiences, and good branding goes one step further to create evangelicals out of customers.

Returning to the concept of experience, we can draw clear lines that distinguish a transaction, a service, and a unique experience. The goal is that you will see how important it is for your business to think in terms of creating unique experiences, not robotically engaging in transactions or providing typical services.

We all have experiences, good and bad, significant and insignificant. The powerful experiences, good and bad, not only stay with us, but they mold us, change us, and dictate what we do and how we live. For example, experiences dictate what and where we'll eat, what clothes we wear, who our friends are, whom we'll marry. Powerful experiences are so significant that you'll go out of your way to duplicate the good ones and avoid the bad ones. When we find a brand that gives us really good experiences, we become loyal. You think of a store, for example, as being *your* store. "My dry cleaners." "My market." "My accountant." Why do you talk about *your* place? Because you feel loyalty to it based on your experiences. When we have positive experiences with a brand, we believe we owe it our loyalty.

Let me draw a simple analogy to retail shopping. If you've had a horrible experience or a series of bad experiences with a store, you'll go out of your way to avoid it. No matter how close and convenient it is—maybe right down the street from your house—you'll drive right past it; you'll go 10 miles out of your way to go to any other store but *that* place. On the other hand, if you've had a wonderful experience or series of powerful experiences with a store, there could be two or three competing stores near your house that sell the exact same stuff, but you'll drive right past them to get to *your* store. Why is it your store? Because you have loyalty to it. You're loyal to the place that is way out of your way, because your loyalty is not about the stuff. It's about the people, the relationships. They've created something so unique, emotional, and memorable that they've developed a relationship with you. If it wasn't for the relationships, you wouldn't go there. You think, I've got it great here. Why take a chance going anywhere else? Besides, they've treated me so well that if I'm going to spend my money in this category, I'm going to spend it with these people. In fact, I'm going to tell everyone I know about this place, because this is the place that will do things right. It's not the stuff, it's the relationships developed from experiences that make a store *yours*.

Our experiences, then, shape our expectations. For example, we expect things to be consistent: The sun rises in the east and sets in the west; there's typically heavy traffic on the freeways in the morning; the grocery store has a wide selection of goods and produce. Almost without exception, our expectations about the future are based on what we experience. Another way to say this is to say that our beliefs are based on a variety of perceptions we have from moment to moment. So, just as businesses that focus exclusively on quarterly profits or sales goals turn customers into mere opportunities for transactions, when businesses focus only on customer expectations, their experience becomes transactional or, at best, just a typical service.

TRANSACTIONAL VERSUS UNIQUE EXPERIENCES

It's true that transactions are experiences, as are services. Insofar as experiences are common to each, we need to focus on what distinguishes one from the other. In Jim Gilmore and Joe Pine's book *The Experience Economy*, we see one approach to differentiating transactions and services from a unique experience. They write, "Experiences are as distinct from services as services are from goods."

Let's start with goods, which most of us commonly think of as being the objects of transactions. A transactional experience is one in which some item or other is exchanged for money. Take, for example, a hot dog. We go to the hot dog stand and pay our money. In return, we get a dog in a bun with mustard and sauerkraut. The experience is a transaction between me and my money, and the server and the hot dog. The relationship between the buyer and seller revolves entirely around the transaction. The customer gives money to the seller, and the seller gives the customer the object. End of story. A seller who offers an experience like this might just as well have said, "I did my job. What more do you want?" Strictly speaking, there *is* no relationship here. For whatever their reasons, many people who work at fast food restaurants seem resentful of being there, and they treat their customers accordingly.

I was at New York's LaGuardia Airport recently one morning and went to the McDonald's on the main concourse for breakfast before my flight. The young woman, about twenty-one, manning the register, had the most miserable expression I've ever seen in my life. As I waited in line, I noticed that she wouldn't smile, say, "May I help you?" or "Thank-you" or even "Hello." All she said, to one customer after another was a monotone, "Next." Now I'm not saying she should have been servile or obsequious, but to provide an exceptional level of service is, to my mind, to behave with dignity. Before I even had the displeasure of placing my order with her, I thought, This is someone who's not going to make it. And if it weren't for the fact that this McDonald's was one of only about two places in the building, the company wouldn't make it, either. They had, essentially, a captive food audience.

But it doesn't have to be this way. I've had experiences at fast-food restaurants that transcended the transactional to become unique. Such experiences were the result of the friendly, dignified, enthusiastic, even charming manner of the person taking my order. Of those people, I always think, They're going to go far in life. About a year ago, I was at the Philadelphia International Airport restaurant waiting for my flight, which had been delayed. Sitting at the bar having a drink, I watched a football game playing on a television over the bar. A woman was sitting down the bar from me who ordered a chicken Caesar salad. She asked the waitress if the chicken was served on the salad itself or on the side. "I'll find out for you," the waitress said and went to the kitchen to ask. A few minutes later, a young man came out from the kitchen and pulled up a seat next to the woman. He looked to be in his late twenties, and from his uniform, I figured he was the cook. He smiled and introduced himself to the woman. "Ma'am," he asked, "did you order the chicken Caesar salad?" "Yes," she answered. "Well, let me ask you a question. How do you want it prepared?" "Well, it really doesn't matter—" "No," he interrupted her. "It *does* matter. You're the customer, and I want you to get what you want. You tell me exactly how you want it, and that's what I'll do. I want to make sure it's perfect." "Okay, I'd like to have the chicken on the salad, and if it's not too much trouble, the dressing on the side." He smiled again and said, "You got it." Then he went back to the kitchen.

A few minutes later, this same cook himself, not the waitress, came back out with the dish. "Do me a favor," he said as he set it down before her. "Take a bite and make sure it's how you want it." When she approved, he turned to go back to the kitchen. As he walked by, I stopped him. "Excuse me," I said, and introduced myself. After we shook hands, I said, "Listen, I have to tell you something. What you just did is something you never, ever see, no matter what kind of restaurant you go to. The level of service you just provided that woman was outstanding, and I'll never forget it." The smile that spread across his face was one of the brightest I'd ever seen. Here was a guy working as a cook in an airport restaurant, probably not making a heck of a lot of money, and probably not fulfilling his life's dream. But what he brought to his work is something that goes well beyond any concern about money or working in a fancy restaurant—where, by the way, the chef might come out to say a brief hello to famous or exceptionally wealthy patrons. "You," I said to the cook, "are going to go very far." He knew it. He didn't think he was being persecuted because he wasn't making $80,000 a year. He knew he had a job that came with certain expectations, and he *shattered* them. The woman who ordered the salad looked at me and said, "I'll never forget this, either!"

These examples show both what a transactional experience is and what an exceptional experience is. The problem is that people on the *serving* side give the customer typical service—only what the customer expects and most times, less than what they expect—instead of a unique, innovative, memorable, emotional experience. They get transactional without even realizing that's what happens. They lose sight of what's truly important, the relationship between them and their customers, of transforming the moment, because their focus is on selling the good, the sales quotas, quarterly goals, and so forth. The difference between the LaGuardia McDonald's cashier and the Philadelphia Airport restaurant cook was that the cook knew exactly what the relationship between brand and customer should be. In fact, I'll bet this guy is still building a powerful brand.

TYPICAL SERVICE VERSUS UNIQUE EXPERIENCE

As I mentioned earlier, we're making distinctions between three types of business models: transactional, typical service, and unique experience. The next level of business model I call typical. It is the model most often called or associated with "service." As with the transactional experience, the interaction between buyer and seller focuses on the customer's standard expectation. Suppose, for example, that I call a customer service department with a problem. My expectation is that the representative will tell me what can be done for me, nothing more and nothing less. The focus in a typical service is on whatever features and benefits the object in question has, and these features and benefits define the parameters of the service. The problem with this attitude toward experience is that its limits are often exceeded by a particular problem. In other words, the scope of the service does not cover the problems people actually have with the product. Here again, the service representative can say, I did my job. What more do you want? But this rhetorical question is precisely what should be genuine! Instead of effectively cutting the experience short, the representative should be seeking to find out what more can be done and then trying to do it.

Part of the transactional and service-only attitudes result from a mistaken belief that you get what you pay for. In other words, the quality of your customer's experience depends on how much money they're spending—or, in the case of the LaGuardia McDonald's cashier, how much you're making. Another way to say this is that experience is treated as hierarchical. Think, for example, about how the luxury goods industry distinguishes an ordinary experience with a luxurious one. The experience of driving a car, for example, is basically the same regardless of whether it's a bottom-of-the-line economy car or a top-of-the-line luxury vehicle. To the extent that you sit behind a wheel and navigate an object that sits on four wheels and covers (mostly) paved ground, you're dealing with experience at a base level. But the quality of the experience changes with the quality of the car. In addition, your own expectation colors, to a certain extent at least, what your experience is like. There are various types of cars on the road because of what people can afford, but also because of what people expect out of their driving experience. Some like to shift gears manually, others want an automatic transmission. Some like to ride high over the road, and some want to "hug" it. The distinctions are too numerous to discuss here, but you get the idea.

The luxury goods industry focuses on a particular type of experience, and associates it with what is elite and exclusive. The attitude is, "You get the experience you pay for," and what you pay for is quality. So the more expensive the item or service, the better it's supposed to be. When people buy into this approach to experience, they set themselves up to settle for a so-called typical customer experience. I argue that *all* customer experiences should and can be unique and extraordinary, whether you're driving through a fast-food restaurant or buying a Mercedes-Benz.

We've already talked about the basics of experience, beliefs, and expectations. Now let's focus on emotions. How you feel about something—how you perceive it—depends on existing beliefs and unique encounters. The first time a child touches a hot stovetop, or a young girl has her heart broken, or a man becomes a father—whatever these experiences are they are powerful, unique, and imprinted on us. They become part of how we feel about ourselves and the world around us. The same is also true about lesser experiences, the sorts of day-to-day experiences we discussed earlier in this chapter. You may form an attachment to a particular activity or thing because it has become habitual. It's sort of like the emotional correlate of always putting your keys in a certain place when you come home, so you don't even think about where they are when you next leave the house; you just go where you left them. Until some *unique* experience changes your perception, your emotions are on a kind of autopilot.

The Unique, Emotional, Memorable Experience

This brings us to the business model of creating a unique experience. It is the model that everyone should follow. This is the level of experience where the relationship between buyer and seller, customer and representative is the focus. Remember that you want to create an evangelical customer. This means that you want to create an emotional connection with your customer. People don't truly get emotional about things, services, or benefits. They may get excited initially, but not emotional at the level that drives loyalty. People get emotional about *people*, people create experiences, and experiences define brands.

Therefore, an emotional experience with a brand is entirely different from a mere service or transactional experience. Indeed, we seek out emotional experiences because we want to make connections with others. What a strange place the world would be if human beings were isolated creatures—isolated from one another and from substantial interaction with the world. We'd be unthinking, unfeeling creatures whose interaction with their environment is mere stimulus response. You don't want a stimulus response brand, which is essentially something like a merely transactional experience. In fact, if all you want is stimulus response from your customer—handing over money and grabbing a bag of something—then transactional experiences are perfect. But I suspect that's the *last* thing you want. Nor do you want a typical service experience, which I liken to interacting with a computer. Computers have a limited range of performance capabilities. They certainly can't surprise you, anticipate what you might like, and then make it happen just so you have a terrific experience. As such, if there's something special you want the computer to do, and it happens to be outside the machine's functional scope, you're out of luck. No, you want a *human* experience. And that's just what we learn about in the next chapter.

CHAPTER 4

FORGET ABOUT ME AND MY STUFF; LET'S TALK ABOUT YOU!

Creating the Ultimate Customer Experience

"THE LION AND THE MOUSE"

Once upon a time, there was a lion, who was fast asleep. As he dreamt about good things to eat, a mouse scurried across him and woke him up.

"Gotcha!" the lion said, snatching the little mouse up into one of his giant claws. "And now I'm going to eat you." He held the mouse by the tail above his gaping mouth, his long, sharp teeth glistening in the sunshine.

"Please, Mr. Lion," the little mouse pleaded. "Do not eat me."

"Why not?" asked the lion.

"Because if you eat me, I cannot help you."

The lion squinted his eyes. "*You* help me?" Then he roared with cynical laughter. "That's a good one."

"No, really," continued the mouse. "It's true. If you let me go today, I promise to help you another day."

The lion paused and carefully considered the proposal. "Well," he said finally. "I doubt very much that someone like you could ever help someone like me, but I am going to set you free, anyway." And true to his word, he set the mouse down.

"I promise to help you!" the mouse cried out as he scurried away. "One day! I promise."

Days turned into weeks, and the lion was cynical about the mouse's promise. Eventually, he forgot all about it. But the little mouse did not forget and waited for just the right moment to arrive.

Then one day, the little mouse's chance finally arrived. The lion walked into a hunter's net and found himself bound up so tight he couldn't move. "I'm done for," the lion thought sadly. Suddenly, the little mouse arrived on the scene and started nibbling away at the nets that held the lion. In short order, the lion was freed.

"I can't believe it!" the lion exclaimed. "I'll never forget you. In fact, I'm going to find all my lion friends and tell them all about what you did for me." And that's just what the lion did.

The moral of the story: Unique, one-of-a-kind experiences change perceptions and change lives!

DEVELOPING RELATIONSHIPS: THE HEART AND SOUL OF BRANDING

This chapter covers one-half of the heart and soul of my branding program, which can be stated in the following simple formula: Create the ultimate level of service for your customer by focusing on relationships, not features and benefits. If you practice the steps discussed here, you will be on your way to building your own powerful, successful brand.

It's true that most people think of service as simply giving the customer what they expect to get, of focusing on a benefit or feature of the sale. In other words, people think of a service as a transaction, an exchange like handing over a dollar and getting some object in return for it. The entire interaction is reduced to the parameters of company policies, regulations, and product performance. But service involves *far* more than a transaction. It's really not service, but *experience*.

"Service" has become a meaningless term to cover everything from a Customer Service desk where people gather to return or exchange products, to being served a summons. Service is not always pleasant or wonderful, so people have to understand that service is not what it used to be. If I lay out $1.50, and someone slaps a hot dog in a bun and slides it carelessly across the counter, that's considered service. Unless you pay a lot of money these days, you get a mere transaction. That's why I distinguish between the transactional nature of service and the relationship establishing nature of experience.

The goal of every interaction with a customer, another business, a friend, relative, and so forth is to create in their minds a specific perception. *That perception comes out of the person's experience.*

If you want to create a brand that is unique, meaningful, and lasting to your customer, you cannot be satisfied with thinking of your customer as an *opportunity* for a transaction, since a transactional experience is mundane and impersonal. In addition, if you want to create a customer who leaves the store an evangelist—someone ready to go out and spread the good news about your brand—you cannot be satisfied with thinking about your *relationship* with your customer as transactional. Transactions are always only the mechanism whereby goods are exchanged. Brands, or powerful, emotional, successful brands on the other hand operate on a higher realm, where *relationships rule* and the ultimate customer *experience* makes your business grow. Providing a service is just doing a job or conducting a transaction. Creating a remarkable experience is branding.

It's true that people have become transactional in their business dealings. Part of this trend, which emerged with mass production, is exemplified by the fast-food industry. You go to the window at the drive-through of a fast-food restaurant anywhere in this country, and you'll experience the pure form of transactional behavior in business. Another, more extreme example of the impersonal service concept has emerged with the explosion of communication technology. E-mail and instant message (IM) software make communication as instantaneous as a phone call, and they are often more time efficient. Nevertheless, these communication devices make people feel disconnected from the experience of human interaction. Human communication is nuanced and variable. In the course of speaking with someone, you may go down several paths, several lines of thought. This is because each speaker contributes something to the process, thereby rendering it dynamic. On the other hand, e-mail exchanges are static. Even instant messages, with all the emoticons and means of expressing emotion and tonal inflection, do not have the same resonance as in-person, or even phone communication. Unfortunately, we've taken the IM and e-mail mindset and have extended it into other areas of our lives, such as our personal and professional lives.

You have a greater chance of botching your communication when you rely on e-mail and instant messaging. In fact, it *far* exceeds miscommunications that arise from direct interaction. Consider the following statement: Ray thinks Tom will succeed. Depending on which word is emphasized, the meaning changes completely:

Ray thinks Tom will succeed. (It's Ray, and no one else who thinks this.)

Ray *thinks* Tom will succeed. (Ray's not entirely certain.)

Ray thinks *Tom* will succeed. (It's Tom, and no one else.)

Ray thinks Tom *will* succeed. (Tom's not succeeding now, but it will happen.)

Ray thinks Tom will *succeed*. (As opposed to fail.)

In face-to-face interactions, there would not be a question about the sentence's meaning, since the person's inflection would make it clear. Face-to-face interactions mean that you have to see another person's point of view, and in so doing, you develop relationships. The result of this lack of interaction and the compassion that personal contact engenders not only hinders our communication skills—unless we're careful—but also leads to the disintegration of your business. For example, the method of connecting with customers almost exclusively by e-mail is one on which one arm of the Apple company relies. I believe it will turn out to be problematic for Apple customers, even those who grew up never knowing a world without personal computers and the Internet. Though I believe Apple's brand is one that's remarkably successful, their reliance on e-mail is, in my view, a misstep, and it shows how even the most successful brands can stumble. Later, we discuss how important it is to continually renew your brand, and Apple's stumble teaches us that we should always be mindful of what we could—and should—do better.

As part of its extended and interrelated product line (including iTunes, iWeb, iPhoto, and Mac Mail), Apple created .Mac. This fee-based web site allows both Mac and Windows users to store, back up, and share files on the Internet. It's a neat idea and, due in large part to the success of related products, iTunes and the iPod, has been very successful for the company.

The problem comes in when you need support. Suppose, for example, that your computer seems to have trouble synching your address book full of e-mail, phone numbers, and physical addresses with your Mac.com account. You can't simply pick up the phone and call Apple unless you've paid for an extended service called AppleCare, and even then, the tech reps can't help you with certain aspects of your Mac.com package. In fact, finding customer support phone numbers on the Mac.com site takes a bit of searching. So, you take the time to go through all the troubleshooting steps you know of, and since you can't get immediate help, you spend a significant amount of time scouring the message boards on mac.com for information about your particular predicament. You can e-mail the dot Mac support staff, but not only do you have to wait at least 12 hours for a response, you don't always get an answer that helps you with your particular problem.

Because technology is impersonal and unemotional, it cannot inspire loyalty. So, not only is technology hurting our communication skills, but it's also diluting the loyalty factor. If there is not a person with whom to interact, you're not going to be loyal; people aren't loyal to products, we're loyal to people. It would not be surprising if, as more mp3 players and music sources flood the market, provided the companies that sell them offer the ultimate customer experience, the popularity of the iPod and iTunes could wane. In Chapter 10, I discuss in more detail the culture that the Apple brand is trying to generate through products like its iPod, but this culture is likely not going to flourish without careful attention to brand cultivation across its product line.

TRANSCENDING THE TYPICAL: MICHELENE, NAYAN, AND RAY

All this is not to say that transaction-style service is inherently bad, but it does not improve your brand. Contrast those types of transactions previously discussed with three remarkable stories about individuals who rose to the level of creating the ultimate customer experience: Michelene, a customer service representative from Verizon Wireless; Ray Coombs, a sales representative from Par Technologies; and Nayan Patel, a franchise owner from Super 8 Motels.

In preparation for a series of keynote presentations I was contracted to make across much of the country for Verizon Wireless, I did a lot of research, which included a visit to their corporate offices, meetings with the marketing staff, visits to their stores, and a couple of hours in one of their call centers. This call center was a huge room with more than 500 representatives. It looked utterly uniform and like a modern-day version of a factory. All the customer service reps were wearing headsets, working in cubes on computers, and taking calls from customers. I had the pleasure of sitting next to one of their customer service reps, a young woman named Michelene, who had personality and charm to spare. She lit the room up with her smile, and I'm certain her smile could be felt over the phone. I sat next to Michelene with my headset on, listening in on her calls.

For the first 20 or 30 minutes the calls she fielded were very simple and very typical: "How do I change my ringer ID?" "Can I have my phone forwarded to my boyfriend's phone?" "What is this charge on my bill?" Michelene handled them all with the highest level of professionalism. She was courteous, friendly, knowledgeable, and charming. And above all, *she always offered more than the customer asked for.* She sent them away feeling wonderful about the experience. In other words, Michelene created in her customers' minds a perception not just of satisfaction but, far more importantly, the perception that she was *the only solution to her customers' problems.* The call she got next illustrates this idea. This was the call that blew me away because, of all my experiences, this was one of the most impressive.

It started out as "The Call from Hell" but finished with the caller believing Michelene was an angel. The first words out of the caller's mouth were, "I'm disgusted with this company! I've never had such poor service in my life! I'm finished with Verizon Wireless! This guy in your store in Manhattan really ticks me off! I want to split my service, and he's telling me I can't do it!" The vitriol dripping from every inflection in this guy's voice was based on a single, very poor experience with one

Verizon employee in a store in Manhattan. As I listened to the caller's complaints, it became obvious that this sales associate in Manhattan had not listened to the customer, had not focused on creating a wonderful experience; certainly he had no intention of building a relationship. Instead, the sales associate had been 100 percent focused on the features, benefits, rules, contract statements, and so on of the customer's wireless package.

I was not alone in my assessment. Michelene also quickly zeroed in on the problem and began offering solutions. Not only that, she went *beyond* solutions. She also offered her compassion, sensitivity to his frustrations, and genuine concern. She quickly and completely solved his problem. *Michelene focused on him as a person and focused on relationship building.* She didn't ignore Verizon Wireless' rules, contracts, and guidelines, but she did put them in their proper place: below the relationship-building process.

First, she said, "I'm sorry, but you've been misinformed. Perhaps the associate is new, or perhaps he misunderstood your question. The fact is, you can split your service." By immediately acknowledging the caller's frustration and offering reasons why the Manhattan associate had been unsuccessful, Michelene was able to establish a rapport with the caller and save the company. But she didn't just leave it there. She didn't simply commiserate. Within five minutes of dealing with Michelene, this man went from experiencing rage to experiencing love! She took him through a process whereby she immediately connected with him, built a rapport, calmed him down until he was ready to listen, and then got him to believe and trust her. That's because, at that point, the call wasn't about splitting service.

What Michelene did next exemplifies what it means to create the ultimate customer experience. She said to him, "Sir, the split takes about 24 hours to activate. Today is Friday and I don't work on Saturdays. However, you've been through a lot and I want to make sure you are completely satisfied, in fact more than satisfied with your Verizon Wireless service. I only live a couple of miles from the office. I'm going to come into the office tomorrow around noon and pull your information up on my computer. Please have your cell phone with you. I'm going to call your cell phone around noon. As soon as you answer it, I'll be able to tell on my computer if in fact the split took place."

There was shocked silence on the other end of the line. Here was a young lady whom he's never met before offering to come in on her day off to help him out! "Michelene," he protested, "I could never ask you to do that, to come in on your day off. You've done enough already." He couldn't believe a woman he'd never met, who works at a company this big, would do something like this.

"You're not asking," she responded. "I'm offering. In fact, I insist. You've already been through enough frustration, and this is the least I can do to mitigate what you've been through."

In that moment, he was converted. An evangelist was born. As I listened in on the call, I thought for sure he was going to drive from New York City up to Rochester to give her a hug.

If it weren't for Michelene's exemplary level of service, the caller would have left that store in Manhattan in a fit of rage and said, "The hell with Verizon Wireless. I'm moving on!" And thereafter, he would have become their most virulent antievangelist in years. Every time he saw someone pull out a phone, he would ask them who their service provider was. If it was Verizon, he'd tell them how awful the company was. I could imagine him saying, "You're not going to believe what happened to me. I used to have Verizon, but let me tell you what horrible service I got." If the relationship between that caller and Verizon wireless had ended in Manhattan, he would have become an enemy of Verizon Wireless. Instead, he made a phone call and met Michelene. She turned an enraged individual into one of the greatest evangelists this company has seen in recent history.

Now here's the real kicker. I tapped Michelene on the shoulder and whispered, "Ask him what he does."

She nodded and said into her headset, "Sir, may I ask what it is you do?"

"Michelene," he said, "You you can ask me anything you want. I'm the chief engineer of the Fox News Building in Manhattan."

Wow! Do you think this man knows a few people? I think this man knows *more* than a few people! Thank goodness he made the call and Michelene saved the situation by creating the ultimate customer experience.

This true story has one very serious, inherent problem that runs rampant in businesses of all sizes. It doesn't matter if you have 50,000, 50, or 5 people in your organization. You can't have some people working at Michelene's level simply to offset the others who work at the level of Verizon's Manhattan store representative. You've got to have *everybody* working at Michelene's level, and when you do, that's when your company becomes the company that is the solution to every customer's problem. Ray Coombs, the Par Technologies sales representative, is another exemplar of an individual coming up with the *only* solution to his customer's problem.

I had the opportunity to give a presentation to Par Technologies about a year ago. Par is a large international company that develops and manufactures point of purchase and cash register technology. They supply most of the fast-food industry; in particular, giants like Burger King and McDonald's. Ray was the Utica, New York-based sales representative for McDonald's.

It so happened that the day of my presentation coincided with an awards banquet at which the company was saying farewell to Ray, who was retiring after 30-plus years with the company. So after I had finished, I stayed around to watch the awards banquet. During the ceremony honoring Ray, a scanned letter was flashed onscreen. It was from a McDonald's senior vice president. After congratulating Ray on his retirement, the letter told him that, "to be perfectly honest with you, we never in our wildest dreams would have thought we'd rely so much on one individual for so much of our business. You're going to be sorely missed." Indeed. The letter from the McDonald's executive was about a man who continually provided an extraordinary service. And here's one story to highlight this fact.

One Sunday morning at about eight-thirty, Ray got a call at home from a McDonald's corporate executive. A franchisee in Worcester, Massachusetts, needed help. His CCU was down, and this meant that all the restaurant's cash registers were down, too. Ray drove up to the factory in Utica and let himself in—against Par corporate policy. As he said later, "I'd rather apologize tomorrow than have to tell my customer I can't help them because it's against the rules." He then put a CCU in his car, drove the 200-plus miles to Worcester, and installed the device. By early that afternoon, the franchise was up and running. If it hadn't been for Ray's priorities and sincere desire to give his customer what he would absolutely love, that franchise would not have had a new CCU until Tuesday, at the earliest. All transactions would have to have been by pencil and paper, and thousands of dollars would have been lost. Yet another exceptional story comes from Sean Wiggins, the director of Business Development at Super 8 Motels. In Covington, Georgia, Super 8 Motel franchise owner Nayan Patel created the ultimate customer experience for an NBC film production crew. They reserved a block of 10 rooms for a few days. When they arrived, the coordinator asked for one set of adjoining rooms so that the crew could store their valuable cameras and equipment, and have easy access to it. "Well," the front desk clerk said, "we don't have adjoining rooms."

Nayan, who was in the office just behind the front desk, came out. "Don't worry, go ahead and do your shoot. When you're done, come see me, and I promise to have a solution for you." When the crew left, he said to his clerk, "Don't ever say, 'We don't, we can't.' Find out whatever the customer needs, wants, and loves, and tell me. Then I'll do everything humanly possible to not just get them what they want, but exceed their expectations." So, when the crew went off for the day's shoot, Nayan hatched and executed a plan. When the crew returned to the hotel about 12 hours later, they were exhausted. When asked what solution the motel owner had come up with, Mr. Patel said, "Come with me." He led them to one of their rooms and opened it up. Inside there was a door that hadn't been there that morning. It opened into the adjacent room. Voilà!

Adjoining rooms. At that point, the NBC contact person said, "I thought you didn't have an adjoining room." With a smile, Nayan responded, "I didn't this morning." Patel had spent the day knocking out part of the wall that connected the two rooms and installing a locking door. Needless to say, the crew was elated, and the 10-room reservation increased to 65 for the week. By exceeding customer expectations—by literally surprising his customer—Patel earned himself brand evangelicals. He did not limit himself to the existing situation—in this case, the physical situation of the rooms—and then try to work within those parameters. Instead, he identified the needs of his customer, and went above and beyond to not just satisfy the need, but to give them a completely unexpected experience.

For more than 20 years, I owned and operated my own marketing and advertising company, RCI, Inc. In addition to creating and sustaining powerful brand identities for our clients with standard advertising and marketing campaigns, we also developed sales, channel communications, CEO programs, and operation management processes. These programs were so innovative and so successful that our clients could not imagine us and our unique services not being a part of their businesses. We did what no other marketing and advertising companies were doing. We were unique to the extent that we became indispensable for many of our clients.

One year, when we were in the midst of putting the next year's budget together for one of our regional clients, a Carrier distributor in North Carolina, we got a call from their Marketing Director, Jodie Noe. "Scott," she implored us. "Please don't be cheap. Don't cut your profit margins down so far that you're going to have a hard time staying in business. You don't do me any good by hurting financially. So, I want you to do what you have to do to make it fair for all concerned, and make enough of a profit for yourself so that you can stay in business for me." This is how indispensable we were to this client. Again, no other agency did what we did.

When I sought new business, I used my agency's uniqueness, what we did for other companies, to secure new clients. I always remember what Chuck Corneu, a good friend and a director at Carrier, told me once. "Scott," he said, "you live or die by your service because you live or die by the grapevine." Those words became not just my company's mantra, but my personal one, too.

These are the ideals in branding. Sadly, the fact is, most Americans are used to subpar, transactional experiences with brands. This, however, is no excuse for a company or an individual to behave accordingly or expect less than stellar experiences. Sometimes we remain loyal to a brand even after the level of service has waned. We want to be loyal, and we give people chances, but there's a breaking point in each of us. Such was my experience with Regis Hair Salon in Syracuse, New York.

For some time, I went faithfully to Regis every month or so for a haircut. I went through a few stylists because each one would keep me waiting for at least 15 minutes. If I had an appointment at two o'clock, I wouldn't get in the chair until two-twenty because the stylist would squeeze someone in before me. I'd tell the stylist that I needed them to stay on schedule. Invariably, they wouldn't. The last stylist who cut my hair did a nice job, and I even drove business her way. But soon enough, the delays began. I told her that my time was important and if I made an appointment, I expected her to honor it. She assured me she would, but lo and behold, the next month, she told me she'd be with me in 20 to 30 minutes. "Okay," I said and walked out. I haven't been back since. Regis' stylists didn't even approach anything remotely resembling the ultimate customer experience; they couldn't even reach the baseline level of meeting a customer's expectations!

BRANDING: IF YOU BUILD IT, THEY WILL COME—BUT YOU'VE GOT TO SUSTAIN IT!

Building a brand is not your only responsibility. You also have to maintain it and be proactive to make things right when they go wrong—especially if you're trying to rebound from a disastrous customer experience. You might remember the story that broke in 2005 about a San Jose, California, Wendy's restaurant customer, Anna Ayala, who claimed to have found a human finger in her chili. It turned out the woman had lied in an attempt to receive a financial settlement from the company. There was nothing wrong with Wendy's chili or their chili making processes. But in the immediate aftermath of the woman's accusation, Wendy's stores in the area suffered greatly. Sales plummeted, and it took some time after Ayala was found to be a scammer for the restaurants to come back. A 2005 cbsnews.com article reported that San Jose area Wendy's alone lost $2.5 million as a result of the incident, and the losses resulted in both layoffs and reduced hours for Wendy's employees. The financial losses were concentrated in the region surrounding the store, but they trickled out to the entire country.

The problem, in my view, was with Wendy's initial response. Rather than going on an offensive by taking to the airwaves to discuss their cuisine and manufacturing processes, they remained silent. Their attitude was, "We'll let the facts resolve the case." Unfortunately, their response was only half what they should have done. Compare Wendy's chili incident with the 1982 Tylenol tampering case, and the syringe found in a Pepsi can just over 10 years later. Johnson & Johnson, Tylenol's parent company, was confronted with a terrible crisis after seven people in Chicago had died from ingesting cyanide-laced Tylenol Extra-Strength. News spread quickly, and there was national panic. *Johnson & Johnson put public safety ahead of company profits* by immediately recalling *all* Tylenol bottles and imploring customers not to buy or take any Tylenol products until they could determine the source of the tampering. Approximately 31 million bottles—about $100 million worth—were recalled. Johnson & Johnson also insisted and proved this could not have occurred at either of their manufacturing plants. This assured the public that the brand was trustworthy. Their willingness to put safety above profits, coupled with their high road tactics in assuring their production integrity scored huge points with the public and investors, and bolstered their brand.

Likewise, in 1993 Pepsi guaranteed its customers that their manufacturing and production processes precluded the possibility that the syringe—or any of the other objects that were later claimed to have been found in cans of Pepsi—had been put in the can by someone affiliated with Pepsi. Not only did the company put out news releases, it also invited news cameras into their manufacturing plants so people could see firsthand that the process was immune to the sort of tampering that had been claimed. Authorities ultimately concluded the claims were hoaxes, but Pepsi's proactive response helped allay consumers' fears in the meantime. And like Tylenol, their proactive high road approach not only saved the brand, but also improved it.

Every day brings new experiences, and with them, new opportunities to create, exercise, or rehabilitate your brand. By reaching out to your customers, you establish relationships that cannot be founded through advertising or marketing campaigns. And these relationships are continually renewed and strengthened through direct, personal contact. In the final analysis, when you create the ultimate customer experience, whether to establish or maintain your brand, or to rescue it from customer antievangelism or espionage, you must perform the unexpected. Reinforce your focus on the brand–customer relationship process, not transactions that merely involve features and benefits. Create a perception in the minds of your customers that your brand is the *only* solution to their problem, not just another choice, and you will establish a loyal, evangelical customer base. Ben & Jerry's ice cream company did just that.

Ben & Jerry's started out in 1978 as a venture between two childhood friends, Ben Cohen and Jerry Greenfield. A year previously, they had completed an ice cream making correspondence course from Penn State—the course had cost $5.00. After borrowing $4,000 and investing an additional $8,000 of their own, the partners opened Ben & Jerry's Homemade ice cream scoop shop in a renovated gas station in Burlington, Vermont. It sounds like an average small business story. And if it hadn't been for the duo's unique brand, it probably would have remained anonymous. But these two were after something far beyond average.

Ten years after serving their first scoop, Ben & Jerry received the Corporate Giving Award from the Council on Economic Priorities for donating 7.5 percent of the company's pretax income to various nonprofit organizations through their Ben & Jerry's Foundation. Not only that, there were more than 80 Ben & Jerry's franchise scoop shops in 18 states, pints of Ben & Jerry's ice cream were distributed to grocery stores across the Northeast, and the company's annual sales for its 10-year anniversary *exceeded $47 million!*

Fast-forward to 2006. Ben & Jerry's is an established brand known and trusted for its superior ice cream, environmental concerns, and commitment to its home state. How the company reached the heights of corporate success—and how it's remained there—is due in large part to the evangelicals the company created. From the beginning, Ben Cohen and Jerry Greenfield created an ice cream, then a store, and then a company that reached out to people. Sure, the ice cream was terrific, and the marketing was ingenious. (Free scoops all day at the scoop shop on its one-year anniversary didn't hurt, and it started a tradition that continues to this day!) But in the end, people reached for Ben & Jerry's because of the experience. Through their unique packaging that promoted their various social works, the company was able to recreate and extend that experience across the country.

From the beginning, the partners struck folks as genuine. We want to create a thriving business, but we want to do good things, too, they seemed to say. When they opened the very first Ben & Jerry's Homemade ice cream scoop shop in Burlington, Vermont, they renovated the former gas station with some help from friends. That summer they held their first free summer movie festival by projecting movies onto the outside wall of the station (now store). Right away, intimacy was established between the shop and members of the community. Ben & Jerry's became the place to hang out.

Even after they had begun distributing to local grocery and mom-and-pop stores and had moved into larger facilities in Burlington, Ben and Jerry continued their commitment to the community. As the business grew, so did employment opportunities for Vermonters. Ben & Jerry's Homemade has remained steadfastly a Vermont company. The milk, the prime ingredient in Ben & Jerry's ice cream, comes from local family farm cows. In addition, the company doesn't compromise on the quality of the ingredients or the manufacturing process. They stopped using Oreo cookies because the product contained lard, and rather than throwing away excess materials, they began feeding a Stowe, Vermont, pig farm ice cream waste.

Okay, you might think. Lots of companies are increasingly environmentally and socially conscious. What's the big deal about Ben & Jerry's, and what's it got to do with creating evangelical customers? Ben & Jerry's isn't simply a company that donates money "on the side." Instead, their social and environmental identity is bound up with their product and their brand; in fact, there's no distinction. This is what makes the Ben & Jerry's experience unique. Here is a company that makes a food product treasured by millions. Not only does Ben & Jerry's promise to make ice cream like we remember from our youth, they *live up to and exceed the ideal.* Every parent wants their children to have truly wholesome ice cream, and that wholesomeness is bound up with the Ben & Jerry's brand.

For example, in 1989 Ben & Jerry's spoke out against Bovine

Growth Hormone (BGH), refusing to use milk from cows that were given the hormone. That same year, they launched Rainforest Crunch. Some of the profits of that ice cream go indirectly toward rain forest preservation efforts. A year later, pints of Chocolate Fudge Brownie were introduced, and the company made sure consumers knew the brownies came from Greyston Bakery in Yonkers, New York. This bakery employs disadvantaged people in the community. Also in 1990, Support Farm Aid was printed on eight million pint containers—which in 2001 were entirely converted to unbleached paperboard, biodegradable Eco-Pint packaging—along with an 800 number people could call to support family farmers. Ben and Jerry even wrote a book, *Double Dip: Lead With Your Values and Make Money* detailing, among other things, their belief that the finest business in the world will, in the future, be evaluated by their values, not their products or services. This makes sense in a number of ways. For example, we know that products are getting better and better. By and large, everything from detergent to cell phones does its job. So what distinguishes one company's product from another? It's not the product that becomes the differentiator, it's the company, what it stands for, and how it treats its employees and citizens. In the case of Ben & Jerry's these values largely define who they are.

As of this writing, Ben & Jerry's Homemade, Inc. has become a public company worth hundreds of millions of dollars. But its status as a giant in the industry—and a publicly owned company—has not meant its brand has altered. In fact, it's the brand that makes this unconventional company as wildly successful as it is. Stockholders "want in" on the company not only because it is profitable, but also because they are themselves evangelicals. They believe in the brand, and they want everyone to know about it.

Creating the ultimate customer experience comes in many forms. This experience can be an individual making a personal connection with you on behalf of a business or the values of a business that the brand represents. In both cases, the experience is emotionally significant to you.

CHAPTER 5

CAN I BORROW YOUR SHOES?

Walking a Mile in Your Customers'— and Your Employees'—Shoes

"THE FROG PRINCE"

One day a princess was playing by the beautiful castle lake with a golden ball. Every time she threw it up into the air, it glistened and shone brilliantly in the sunlight. The princess was very happy with her beautiful golden ball! But then she threw it too high, the shining sun blinded her briefly, and she lost sight of it. When it started back toward earth, she could not catch it and it fell into the lake. "Oh, no! Oh, no!" she cried, seeing that the lake was too deep for her to reach the ball. Indeed, the water was so dark she could not even see where the lovely globe had landed. With tears streaming down her face, the princess despaired of ever retrieving her valuable toy.

Just then, a voice asked, "Princess, what ails you?" She looked up to see it was an old frog, its mottled skin glistening in the sunlight as it bobbed in the water before her. "Oh!" she said, startled by the voice. Soon, however, she regained her composure. "I have lost my golden ball, Mr. Frog. It is my favorite toy in the whole world. Oh, it cannot be lost! What I wouldn't do to have it back!"

The frog blinked twice and said, "I can get it for you."

Immediately, the princess's face brightened, and she squealed, "Yes! Please do!"

The frog cleared his throat. "All right. But what will you give me in return?"

Delighted, she offered him riches. "Anything! Anything you want—except, of course, my precious golden ball. My father, the king, has riches beyond your wildest imagination. We can pay you handsomely."

The frog cleared his throat once again, and hopped out of the lake and onto the bank beside her. "I do not need or want riches. I want only to be loved. I have been so terribly lonely here for so long. If you love me and keep me for your companion and let me sit next to you at the table, that would be enough for me."

She quickly agreed, her eyes staring into the deep waters of the lake. "Is that all you request?" With a wave of her hand, she said, "Yes, of course. I will love you and let you sit next to me at the table."

With that, the frog jumped back into the lake, emerging moments later with her ball. Before he'd even gotten back up onto the bank, the princess screamed with delight and snatched the ball out from between his webbed fingers. Then she left without keeping her promise. "Wait! Wait!" the frog cried after her, but she skipped away without even once looking back. Consider what that ugly creature wants? she thought. Never!

That evening the princess told her father the king about how she'd lost her golden ball but had managed to retrieve it. In every detail, the story was accurate, except she never once mentioned the frog. Just then, there was a knock at the castle door. In came the frog. As soon as the princess saw the frog, she was enraged. "He's slimy and disgusting!" she screamed. "Send him away at once!"

At first, the king was going to obey her wishes, but the frog quickly told his story. Turning to his daughter, the king asked, "Is this true?" Her downcast eyes told him everything he needed to know.

Much to her dismay, the princess was forced to keep her promise, which she would never have done otherwise. Not only would she not have considered what the frog might like, she would not have considered him at all! Grudgingly, she sat the frog next to her at the table, where he dined heartily.

Then, again at her father's command, she had to give up her most comfortable bed so her new companion could sleep soundly. When he asked for water, the princess stamped her foot and grabbed him from under the covers. "You're a smelly, ugly frog!" she screamed, and threw him against the wall. In that very moment, he turned into a handsome prince.

"If only you had kept your word," the deep-voiced prince said sadly. "If only you had considered my feelings for just a little while." He said no more, heartbroken as he was that the princess would be so callous. Then he left the castle, and the princess never saw him again.

The moral of the story: "When you change the way you look at things, the things you look at change."—Dr. Wayne Dyer.

I AM MY CUSTOMER

Taking another's viewpoint as your own is not an easy thing to do. After all, we're intimately connected only to our own thoughts, feelings, and sensations. It's perfectly natural for us to approach the world from our own perspective. But it's crucial for all of us to be able to change our perspective, to be able to walk in another's shoes. In fact, that's exactly what you need to do. You need to look at your customer and say to yourself, If I was my customer right now, what would I love to have from me? What would I love to have but think is impossible, that there's no way I'm going to get? Then, *do it!*

Changing your perspective—your attitude—about your business, your employees, and your customers is crucial to the success of your brand. Running a business or a department of any size isn't a simple endeavor, nor is working for an organization with goals and objectives to meet. The hours are long, competition is tough, and there are no guarantees that all your hard work will pay off. In the midst of the hectic pace and mountains of work you have to conquer every day, it's easy to lose sight of your most important assets: your customers, your employees, and your fellow workers. If, however, you keep them at the forefront of your concerns, the results will be both tangible and long lasting. When you change your perspective to deliver uncommon experiences—to deliver the impossible—you reap tremendous rewards. But you have to begin to see your business through the eyes of your customers—and, as we'll also see, everyone in your organization.

Before considering what it's like to walk in your customer's

84

shoes, think about what you experience when you're a customer. This is easy enough to do. After all, when you're not busy running your own business, you are some *other* business' customer. Envision the experiences you value when you walk into a store, a restaurant, or call a service department. The interaction at every level is significant. Everything matters, from how it feels when you drive up to the business and walk inside to how you're treated by the staff. Or if your entire interaction is phone-based, it matters how long it takes for your call to be answered, to how difficult the phone tree is to negotiate, to how many representatives it takes to help you, to how you're treated by each one. Are you, the customer, treated as an essential component of the business' success or a mere distraction to getting business done? You, the customer, should feel welcomed, respected, liked, and even loved. These are the first steps you take when you and your employees walk in your customer's shoes.

You should also step outside of your own business and your own role as proprietor, manager, or employee to walk in your own shoes as an average customer—not just the customer you've targeted through market research. Make a conscious effort to be a customer at a competitor's business—especially one known for their exceptional customer relations—and take notes. Then compare the results with your own business. This simple market research focuses your attention on individuals, not demographics. We know that individuals are distinct, unique beings who, though they share a variety of interests and needs in common with others, still perceive the world through their own individual senses. This means you have got to be alert to variation in, as it were, customer shoe size!

YOUR CUSTOMERS ARE NOT CLONES! AVOID THINKING EXCLUSIVELY IN TERMS OF A CORE CUSTOMER

But can you possibly please everybody all the time? Some marketing experts will tell you that you should determine who your core customer is based on profiles such as age, race, income, profession, geographic location, and more—and work to satisfy him or her. For instance, Carrier also owns Bryant, another heating and cooling systems company. A number of years ago, each was marketed very differently. The Carrier customer was thought to be a professional who loved fine food and dining out, drove a BMW, and lived in an upscale neighborhood. The Bryant customer, on the other hand, was considered more working class, someone who loved NASCAR and chewed tobacco. And although the Carrier and Bryant products are virtually identical, they ran their advertising campaigns for each company based on these demographics—and failed miserably. They tried to create a demographic for the Bryant brand that just didn't exist. People want the same things. In the summer they want to be cool and comfortable and not pay too much. You don't have to be an upscale, wealthy corporate honcho to want to have a Carrier compared to a Bryant.

This sort of thinking is incomplete, and as such, somewhat misguided. It focuses not on customer experience, but solely on customer expectation, specifically, core customer expectation. In other words, if your focus is on satisfying your core customer, you're less likely to be interested in creating a unique experience than you are in simply meeting the expectation your core customer already has—or you assume they have based on some sort of research, such as a focus group or standard survey. Of course, you do need to find and understand your core customer base, but you don't want to approach your world from that perspective only, since your business is not exclusively about your core customer. More important, it's dangerous to think of your core customers as clones of each other based on market research. Remember, we're unique individuals, and our perceptions of our experiences are not all uniform. We're not all cows eating the same hay! The story of Song Airlines is a good example of focusing too heavily on a core customer.

Owned and operated by Delta, Song was the low-price, leisure air carrier that started up in April 2003. It took its last flight in April 2006 before its aircraft were incorporated into Delta's fleet. Facing competition from low-cost carriers Jet Blue and Southwest, and still reeling from the effects of 9/11, Delta spun off Song Airlines. It also had to create an entirely new identity for the new carrier so that Song would not be synonymous in travelers' minds with Delta. Delta's previous attempt at a low-fare carrier was Delta Express, which did not survive. Thus, in its new venture, Delta had to make sure that Song Airlines would have a unique, standalone brand. Song executives knew they needed to find a niche customer for their fleet of 36 airplanes.

After extensive market research, Song's core customer was found, and their brand was created around it. The "discount diva" was an upwardly mobile, professional woman between the ages of thirty-five and fifty-four, who makes the majority of travel decisions and arrangements in her family. What she wanted was a return to style in travel, but at an affordable price and with family-friendly amenities.

The service itself was unique among airlines. It boasted a terrific in-flight entertainment system, offered organic meals—including organic baby food—and comfortable leather seats. The airline even developed a pink martini, with 20 percent of the proceeds going to the Avon Breast Cancer Crusade.

Creative director Andy Spade, who is also the husband of successful accessories designer Kate Spade and co-founder and CEO of Kate Spade Designs, was hired to spearhead the advertising end of Song's marketing process and to develop Song's brand identity. That process included a Song in the City concept store in Manhattan, in which people could have the "Song experience," which included food tasting and entertainment. There was also media coverage of Song's partnerships with well-known chef Michel Nischan, who created the airline's organic food program, and fitness authority David Barton. In connection with these marketing elements, Spade developed television commercials that reflected the Song experience, which included the organic meals and irreverent personality that was meant to be uniformly unusual. "We're going to create a campaign for Song that's spirited, that delivers on the benefits that we think are most important. Do it in a way that is emotional. Do it in a way that is optimistic because we believe that is part of the Song ethos," Spade told PBS's documentary series Frontline in 2004.

A combination of air travel and lifestyle brand, Song advertisements emphasized style, health, and entertainment. In one ad, for example, a pop tune plays in the background on a bright, sunny day. Giddy laughter comes from playful, attractive women, men, and children carrying kites who emerge like blossoming flowers on a hill covered with lush green grass, daisies, and a large, shady tree. The people are running and jumping, full of joy. Once they pass by, the camera pans up to the sky and the word "happy" appears. An entire sentence forms around it so the text reads "Now boarding happy people, fresh organic meals, everyday low fares, DISH satellite network tv." The airline's tagline is "Let yourself fly." If we didn't already know that "everyday low fares" refers to the cost of airline tickets, we'd have no way of knowing we'd just seen an advertisement for an airline. But the point, according to Spade, was not to sell an airline, but to sell an idea that, in turn, was based on market research.

Given the meticulous market research and above-average service, why did Song stop singing? Song could not deliver on its brand promise. The food, entertainment, and overall service were all good, but its core customer was not a real person; it was a marketing Frankenstein, an amalgamation of market research. The airline had built its brand around this core customer, and it just wasn't sufficient to keep the airline aloft. Another way to say this is that the lyrics of Song just didn't resonate. Since there is no reality to "a core customer," there could be no reality to the brand. It was all superficial persona. As we see in Chapter 8, brands cannot be sustained in this way. Market research will *never* yield the elements of an excellent brand.

If, on the other hand, your focus is on creating an extraordinary experience for your customers—one customer at a time—there is no more customer hierarchy in terms of the unique customer and all the rest. Moreover, there is no more cloning of your core unique customers, as if they'll all want the same things. Most companies that do think they focus on customer service tend to focus not on the individual, but on products, benefits, and services. Though it's true that businesses need to know the core customers' perceptions of current product, service, and benefit offerings, and it's true that businesses need to know what sorts of product problems, limitations, and shortcomings need to be addressed, this is not what a unique customer experience involves. Instead, to truly walk in your customers' shoes, you need to be open to what moves them emotionally. You need to view the interaction between you and them from their perspective, not yours.

BE YOUR CUSTOMERS AND EMPLOYEES: YOU CAN FIT INTO *ANY* SIZE SHOE!

Perhaps a very personal example will help you understand even better why this point is significant. Each of us has had the following experience at some time in our lives: You come home from work tired and grumpy. You've had a rough day at the office, traffic was bumper-to-bumper all the way home, and all you want to do when you get home is lie back on the sofa and kick your feet up. But as you walk up to the door, your children come out to greet you, rush into your arms, and want to tell you all about their day. "Okay, okay," you say, absently patting their heads, "in a minute." Then your spouse greets you, and you grumble something about needing to unwind, and you disappear into your own world. *It's all about you.* But how do you think your children and your spouse feel? Or maybe *you* are the child or the spouse who is dismissed. Aren't you disappointed?

90

Now rewind the scene. Put yourself in your children's shoes. I don't care what sort of day you had because guess what? Your kids don't care, and neither do your customers. Your kids only care about being with you, and your customers only care about brands overdelivering on their promises. Maybe you're even sick with a fever when you arrive home, but put yourself in your children's shoes, anyway. Ask yourself, If I was my child looking at me *right now*, what would I love from me at this moment? I guarantee you that you *will not* simply pat your child on the head and say you'll listen to them in a few minutes. Nor will you float by your spouse to go unwind somewhere else in the house. I promise you will change the way you approach that situation.

Now that we understand how important it is to walk in your customers' shoes, everyone in your organization needs to feel the same way; they need to be on board with this philosophy. Unfortunately, too many companies treat their employees like they're mere cogs in the company machinery. As a result, it's difficult to get your employees emotionally committed to your brand. And who can blame them? You know the expression, "In order for me to win, you have to lose." It seems a common refrain in business, especially retail. For consumers to buy low-cost products, manufacturers have to make goods cheaply, and suppliers have to sell cheaply to the retailer so that the retailer can sell items cheaply to the customer. In the process, from manufacturing to the store that sells the items, workers' wages are systematically and persistently depressed. How else could things be sold so cheaply while the retailer and everyone else on down the line makes enough to stay in business—or in the case of giants like Wal-Mart, billions of dollars in annual profits?

The Industrial Age had its assembly line workers. The Consumer Age has retail workers who are paid so poorly they often have to work two and three jobs to make ends meet. In between, especially after World War II, was a seeming golden age of middle class stability and prosperity. If, on the other hand, you extend your ultimate customer experience to your employees, you will create a golden brand.

In general, employers have little loyalty to their employees, and employees feel little loyalty to their employers. The result is a transactional relationship between employee and employer: Each employee is to be valued solely for what can be had from him or her, while each employer is to be valued solely for the same reason. Implicit in this transactional notion of value is the idea that relationships are limited to means. In other words, neither the employee nor the employer is viewed as having inherent worth.

Given that the employer is historically in a position of power, the negative consequences of treating employees as mere cogs in the business' machinery typically extend to the customer. We've already seen that business practices that view relationships as transactional fail to build sustainable brands. Recall, too, that if we trace this relationship back, we might find that one of the causes of the transactional attitude is a business' myopic commitment to quarterly profits and, when a company is public, shareholder profits.

In opposition to this environment is Costco's practice of employee retention. As the United States' fifth-largest retailer, Costco's low-price approach to merchandise looks a lot like that of rival Sam's Club and Sam's multibillion dollar parent company, Wal-Mart. And though Costco's overall earnings pale in comparison to Wal-Mart's, Costco has not received consistently negative press about aggressive business practices and employee relations. Although Wal-Mart is a financially successful company, I believe that Wal-Mart's poor business practices will eventually destroy their brand, while Costco's brand will continue to strengthen.

These days, there is much talk about the "big box" retailers squeezing suppliers and workers in order to offer the consumer the steepest discounts—and shareholders the biggest profits. But one of the fastest growing retail companies in the United States is bucking this trend. Costco Wholesale Corporation, a general merchandise company that sells high quality, low-cost items from mayonnaise to automobile tires to crystal chandeliers is doing what not many major retailers are doing: making profits while maintaining customer and employee loyalty.

The business operates on a high volume, limited brand model. Businesses and individuals pay a nominal membership fee and in return can buy items individually or in bulk at discounted prices. Its success is due in no small part to a savvy business model that delicately balances customer, employee, shareholder, and supplier needs. In addition, Costco does not spend money on advertising—a rarity in any business—but chooses to save the 2 percent it would spend to instead reinvest in the company. Nor does the company have a public relations department, instead leaving the evangelizing to their loyal customers, employees, and shareholders.

A crucial component of Costco's success is employee loyalty, which translates to employee evangelism. In a 2006 interview on ABC's *20/20*, Costco CEO Jim Sinegal said, "Imagine that you have 120,000 loyal ambassadors out there who are constantly saying good things about Costco. It has to be a significant advantage for you." Costco has the lowest employee turnover rate in retail. Costco's CFO Richard Galanti says, "From day one, we've run the company with the philosophy that if we pay better than average, provide a salary people can live on, have a positive environment and good benefits, we'll be able to hire better people, they'll stay longer and be more efficient." This is fairly unique and telling, especially given that the tradition of long-term employment has all but disappeared over the past 20 years.

Costco takes seriously its commitment not only to the immediate customer experience of product savings, it also sees the importance of creating a stable environment for its employees, and this affects the overall brand. The average wage for a Costco employee is more than 40 percent higher than its closest competitor, Sam's Club. Employees say they want to work at Costco until retirement—a rare expression of employee satisfaction and loyalty.

Moreover, Costco employees receive excellent benefits. The company contributes 3 percent of each employee's salary to the worker's 401(k) plan at the second year of employment, and this increases to 9 percent after 25 years. In addition, part-time employees are eligible for health insurance after six months of employment, the company insurance plans cover most dental expenses, and 85 percent of Costco employees have health insurance, while only half of Wal-Mart and Target employees are covered.

According to a July 17, 2005 *New York Times* article by Steven Greenhouse entitled "How Costco Became The Anti-Wal-Mart," "Costco's health plan makes those at many other retailers look Scroogish." That same article quotes Deutsche Bank analyst Bill Dreher complaining that ". . . it's better to be an employee or a customer than a shareholder." That may not be entirely true, since Costco's stock price has continued to rise even while other retailers' prices have fallen. Emme Kozloff, a Sanford C. Bernstein & Company analyst, complained that, although Sinegal is "right that a happy employee is a productive long-term employee . . . he could force employees to pick up a little more of the health care burden." At the time of publication, Costco workers were paying 8 percent of health care costs compared to the retail average of 25 percent.

But Costco CEO Jim Sinegal's approach to employee relations is neither divisive nor unfriendly to shareholders. There is no reason to think that a successful and sustainable brand—in this case a retail brand—is one that elevates profits over customers or employees. Sinegal says, "On Wall Street, they're in the business of making money between now and next Thursday. . . . I don't say that with any bitterness, but we can't take that view. We want to build a company that will still be here 50 and 60 years from now." One way to achieve such longevity is through loyal employees. In fact, the numbers bear out the business savvy of keeping employee turnover rates low. Thousands of dollars are lost every time a new employee has to be hired: from notification of open positions to recruiting, interviewing, hiring, and training. According to a 2004 *Business Week* study, Costco employees are more productive than their counterparts at Wal-Mart, and part of the reason can be traced back to retention. Retention is the result, in large part, of Costco treating its employees like customers. Sinegal doesn't *say* this exactly, but his actions speak volumes. He understands employee value.

The effects of Costco's approach to employees ripple outward. According to Sinegal, Costco shoppers appreciate the fact that the low prices they pay do not come at the expense of workers' wages and benefits. Indeed, the relationship between Costco and its employees becomes an important feature of the relationship between Costco and the customer. Given this brand approach, it should be no surprise that Sinegal's salary is less than $1 million a year as CEO—bonuses included. This sort of salary is unheard of among any large company, let alone one that is publicly traded. Of course, his personal wealth is considerable—upwards of $150 million, according to the *Times* article—given his shares of Costco stock. Sinegal notes, "I've been very well rewarded. I just think that if you're going to try to run an organization that's very cost-conscious, then you can't have those disparities. Having an individual who is making 100 or 200 or 300 times more than the average person working on the floor is wrong." This sort of grounded-in-reality attitude extends to his own brand of customer relations: accessibility. In the same *20/20* interview previously cited, Sinegal says, "If a customer's calling and they have a gripe, don't you think they kind of enjoy the fact that I picked up the phone and talked to them?"

This sort of thinking, combined with the fact that Costco's promise to employees is realized in the company's approach to employee wages, benefits, and shares in the company's profits, means that the unique experience of the employees is passed on to the customer. Thus the Costco brand is integrated. Customer benefits do not occur at the cost of employee benefits.

Low product prices do not occur at the cost of supplier and manufacturer profits. This latter situation is reflected in the Costco warehouse model. Rather than selling numerous brands, as Wal-Mart does, Costco stocks fewer types, thereby increasing the sales volume for each brand. This, in turn, allows Costco to get bulk discounts from their suppliers without digging deeply into their own profits.

It's true that part of the unique customer experience includes knowing that Costco values its employees. But there are other tangible and intangible benefits. One is the Costco "treasure hunt." Among the everyday items sold in bulk are treasures, like fine wines and jewelry, the newest in television technology, and luxury handbags—all brand names, and all typically outside the price range of most Costco shoppers. To find Waterford crystal at Costco is extraordinary and part of the excitement of being a Costco member. It also reinforces the idea that Costco is not in the business of selling cheaply made goods. Among the intangible benefits is what the Costco customer feels about the Costco experience. According to one shopper interviewed for the same 2006 *20/20* story on Costco, "This is the best place in the world. It's like going to church on Sunday. You can't get anything better than this. This is a religious experience." Talk about customer evangelism!

What the Costco brand has accomplished since its first warehouse opened in Seattle, Washington, in 1983 is almost entirely unique among retailers. Some high-end stores like Nordstrom are also committed to their employees, but of the big box retailers, Costco is unique.

But Costco is not alone in its unique commitment to employees and customers. In North Carolina, SAS Institute, Inc. is a statistical analysis software (SAS) company that offers unlimited sick days, encourages employees' family members to come and eat lunch at the company, and discourages working late. When most of us imagine what working for a technology company is like, we shudder. People practically live in their cubicles, taking only short breaks before returning to hunch over their keyboards typing out code. SAS breaks the mold of today's technology business model.

The SAS campus outside Raleigh is idyllic. There is day care for employees' kids, world-class athletic facilities, walking trails, and an excellent cafeteria. While employees at many companies seek to get as much as they can while they can, SAS employees seem satisfied—and loyal to company founder and president Jim Goodnight. For nine straight years, *Fortune* magazine has ranked SAS as one of the 100 Best Companies to Work For. For each of the past 29 years, the company has posted increased revenues.

Goodnight and colleagues at North Carolina State University originally developed software to assist statisticians who were analyzing agricultural data. Then he went on to develop other statistical analysis software, and SAS was born. Now the company's software is used by companies as diverse as Marriott hotels and Pfizer pharmaceuticals, and by the U.S. government. Marriott uses software in its frequent visitor program, while Pfizer uses the statistical software in its development of new drugs. The U.S. government enlists the software to calculate the Consumer Price Index. And even though the company's software is ubiquitous among companies and organizations that sift through voluminous amounts of data to find and understand patterns, SAS is probably the least well-known software company in the world. In 2005 SAS earned $1.68 billion.

Be Your Customers and Employees

How does a company become so successful while walking in its employees' shoes? SAS is privately owned by Goodnight and his N.C. State colleague John Sall, so there are no stock options, and the salaries are competitive but not extraordinary. Still, employees are happy. That's because they're treated well. Moreover, although Goodnight has considered taking part of the company public to, among other things, reward employees who have been loyal to SAS while colleagues at publicly owned companies have built wealth through stock options, he won't lose employees' loyalty if he doesn't.

Among other SAS policies that reflect a deep understanding of an employee's needs, there's no limit on sick days, and employees can stay home to care for family members who are ill. To encourage employees to have a life outside work, the day ends at six o'clock when the campus gates are locked. Not only does the company provide a full-service gym free of charge, it also boasts outside soccer and softball fields. The company also has a health clinic and various coordinators and social workers to help employees with personal issues. There is even a company art group headed by an artist originally hired to produce paintings expressly for the company. As Goodnight says, "I believe that a person's surroundings have a lot to do with how a person feels. We try to have nice surroundings here."

It's worked. According to a 1998 fastcompany.com article on SAS, the employee turnover rate for that year was just 3.7 percent. Clearly, employees are fiercely loyal to SAS. The idea behind the largesse is that it's good business. Just as Costco saves money by retaining workers, so also does SAS. For example, the company started its day care facility when it realized it was losing female employees who chose having children over a career.

These women were valuable employees the company did not want to lose. A day care facility made the most sense. The attitude at SAS toward its employees is one of appreciation, an attitude that's reciprocated by SAS employees. There is a level of accountability at SAS that emerges not out of fear, but out of interest in doing the work and respecting the company that treats its employees so well. Not only that, but both Goodnight and Sall—and their various department managers—are doing the same work as the employees who write the software. This means that everyone is "in it together," rather than a few people overseeing the rest to make sure the job gets done. Though this particular model might not work in every business environment, it exemplifies the "walking in your employees' shoes" attitude I've been advocating.

At the highest levels of a corporate hierarchy, then, walking in your employees' shoes is not impossible. It's not, however, without its difficulties. Back in the 1980s, businessman Ross Perot engaged in a very public battle with General Motors. At the time, he was chairman of Electronic Data Systems, a company that had been bought out by General Motors Corporation two years previously. He was also GM's largest individual stockholder and a company director. When GM announced a series of plant closings in 1986, Perot was not pleased. He believed part of his role as a director in the company was to protect the interests not only of the stockholders, but also of the customers, dealers, and employees. In a *New York Times* story from that year entitled, "G.M. Closings Surprise Perot," he is quoted as saying, "I always hoped we could get the job done without closings," he said, adding, "I grew up in a world where good, decent people had it tough and had to look hard for work." To Perot, it was GM's fault that people were going to be laid off. Specifically, poor management had led to a lapse in GM's competitiveness. Eventually, Perot sold his interests in GM and started a new computer company.

Much of the focus of this chapter has been on how companies walk in their employees' shoes. It is an important approach in the process of changing your perspective to deliver exceptional customer experiences. Given the freedom to do their jobs to the best of their already exceptional abilities, SAS employees are able to focus their energies on making the best possible software for their customers. SAS also incorporates a significant number of customer suggestions into its product improvements, which means their customers are being heard.

Of course, we already know that people like Verizon's Michelene are walking in their customers' shoes every day. And it's not just the "feet on the ground," the employees in closest contact with customers, who are stepping into those shoes. Corporate heads like Costco's Sinegal and SAS's Goodnight are as concerned about their customers' perceptions of their brands as they are concerned about their employees. Another example of this is eBay's CEO Meg Whitman.

Since Whitman took over as president and CEO in 1998, she has led the way in working from a different kind of business model. According to a *U.S. News* story in 2005 entitled "Keeping A Gentle Grip On Power," "Whitman has created a radically more democratic company, a model organization in which the collective intelligence and enthusiasm of its 157 million customers determine and drive the daily actions of its 9,300 employees." eBay connects sellers to people who want to buy and are willing to compete for the privilege. A cross be-tween garage sale, flea market, and auction house, people sell everything from jewelry to computers, paintings to cars. The connection between customer and the eBay brand is almost palpable. As Whitman says, the collaboration between customer and brand is The Power of All of Us.

Whitman's leadership style reflects the perspective change that makes it possible to step into her customers' shoes. Rather than think of herself as the person in charge, controlling every-thing that happens in and to the company, she characterizes herself as being in a collaborative partnership with its members and customers. In doing so, her ears are open to listening to what others have to say, and her mind is open to trying some-thing new. This openness requires a great deal of trust—specifi-cally, trust that customers will do the right thing. The foundational idea that customers are basically good comes from Pierre Omidyar.

The creator and chairman of eBay and self-described "tech-nologist" believes in "trying to make the world a better place." According to a December 2001 interview with *Business Week*, Omidyar began eBay as an online Pez dispenser–trading venue for his then-girlfriend (who is now his wife). It quickly grew well beyond Pez trading. An important feature of the online auction site was that buyers and sellers communicated di-rectly. What makes Omidyar's initial vision and subsequent site development unique among brands is that he never lost sight of the importance of stepping into his customers' shoes—be they buyer or seller. And just as importantly, he cultivated and encouraged the same attitude in the eBay member community.

BE YOUR CUSTOMERS AND EMPLOYEES

Omidyar's vision was "about how people should treat one another, and about how most people feel they should treat one another." From the beginning, he had to advocate and explicate that vision, because it wasn't always foremost in his customers' minds. For example, sometimes out of fear that they would get ripped off because the transactions were all completed entirely online, customers would be "a little quick to react and didn't give a lot of thought to the fact that most people are honest and good and trying to do the right thing." In response to this attitude, Omidyar suggested taking something of a time out. "Put yourself in the other person's shoes," Omidyar would advise. "Maybe they don't turn on their computer every day. Don't jump to negative conclusions, maybe there's a reasonable explanation." In almost all cases, eventually I would get back an e-mail saying, "Oh, you were right, everything's fine." By counseling the community members early to put their best selves forward, Omidyar created a brand that eBay members embraced as their own.

Another way in which Omidyar practiced walking in his customers' shoes was creating an evaluation system in which users monitored one another's practices. He says he learned that putting the power of policing the site in the customers' hands led to a system called the Feedback Forum. This not only gave users the power to monitor one another, it also made them responsible for their own conduct. Anyone who wants to give a buyer or seller a bad review has to think seriously about the impact it might have. By placing his trust in the essential goodness of his customers, Omidyar, along with CEO Meg Whitman, was able to steer the company in a remarkably profitable direction. Though the community is not 100 percent self-governing, the principle behind Omidyar's idea continues to resonate.

In addition to establishing his value system for the company and letting customers be responsible for their own conduct, Omidyar also "wanted to create an efficient market and a level playing field where everyone had equal access to information." So he went straight to the customers, taking their suggestions for improving the site, and then implementing them. In the *BusinessWeek* interview, Omidyar goes on to say, "From a customer-loyalty point of view, I learned later, it's wonderful when you write into a company, and somebody who's responsible responds to your e-mail and says, 'You know what? That's a really good idea. Let me work on that.' And then in a couple of days, you actually see the changes on the site. That gives you, as a user, a sense of ownership of the site. And it makes you a very loyal customer." Talk about walking in your customers' shoes!

When Whitman joined the company, she not only continued Omidyar's customer-based philosophy, she has, as we have seen, brought her own collaborative style of leadership to the position. Still known at the time as Auction Web, eBay was still a small company with only about a dozen employees when Whitman arrived. With her stewardship, and based on the unique business model established by Omidyar, eBay survived the dot com bust. In addition, Whitman has developed and extended that business model to help make eBay the fastest growing business in the history of U.S. businesses.

It's true that part of the nature of eBay lends itself to the customer shoes idea I've been pursuing in these pages. With the exception of banning altogether the sale of certain items like firearms and alcohol, eBay does not control inventory or merchandising.

When you walk in your customers' and employees' shoes, you enlarge yourself. Your perspective widens, and so does your concern about what's important. The benefits you receive from changing your perspective will far exceed those reaped from a narrower vision that includes only the bottom line.

CHAPTER 6

GET OVER YOURSELF!

We're Not as Great as We Think We Are

"THE FOX AND THE CROW"

A wily fox spied a crow in a tree branch above where he sat shading himself against the afternoon sun. The fox was very hungry, and he noticed that the crow carried in her beak a large, lovely slab of cheese. Drooling with hunger, the fox thought, I must have that for myself! Looking up at the crow, he said in his most velvety voice, "What a beautiful and noble creature I see above me. Her every aspect is a sight to behold, and I am enraptured. But, I wonder, does her voice sound as sweet as her looks are lovely?"

The crow, which had been setting herself to the task of eating the delicious cheese, was intrigued by what she had heard. She thought to herself, Indeed, I am as lovely in all respects as this gentleman believes me to be, but how should he know if I do not prove it to him myself? With that, she opened her beak and belted out a giant "Caw! Caw!" She knew the fox would find her dulcet tones as inspiring and attractive as her looks. But at that very moment the cheese fell from her beak and into the waiting mouth of the fox below. In a single gulp, the cheese was devoured, and the fox's empty stomach was full and satisfied.

Trotting away, the fox smiled up at the dejected crow. "My dear, your voice *is* lovely, but your *wit* is dull!"

The moral of the story: Get over yourself! Stop thinking you are wonderful and preening over your brand, and start building it!

THE LAKE WOBEGON EFFECT

It's true. We're not as terrific as we think we are. That's because we suffer from what one of my favorite authors, Harry Beckwith, refers to as the Lake Wobegon Effect. Lake Wobegon is the fictional town created by writer and satirist Garrison Keillor and featured on his variety radio show *The Prairie Home Companion*. Lake Wobegon is the place where "the women are strong, the men are good-looking, and the children are above average." Keillor was no doubt onto something. As human beings, we suffer from the Lake Wobegon Effect. In the late 1980s, West Virginia pediatrician and education activist Dr. John Cannell released the findings of a study that became known as the Lake Wobegon Effect. In it, he concluded it was statistically impossible for average student test scores in each of the 50 states to be above the national norm. Yet this was exactly what every state in the union was claiming. His suspicions were first piqued when his own state released the results of its Comprehensive Test of Basic Skills (CTBS). Apparently, despite the fact that West Virginia, which had the highest percentage in the nation of adults without college degrees, was close to the bottom in the results of the American College Testing (ACT) and had the second-lowest per capita income, West Virginia students tested above-average at every grade level!

Yes, it's true. We all think we're better than we really are. We all overestimate our talents and skills. Consider our driving skills. We think we're excellent, or at least above average, drivers. It's *everybody else* on the road who are causing problems. It's *everybody else* who can't drive. Those people who drive and talk on the cell phone at the same time? They're dangerous but we, *we* know how to multitask. You might recall George Carlin's comment about our inflated views of our driving skills: "Have you ever noticed that anybody driving slower than you is an idiot, and anyone going faster than you is a maniac?" Sound familiar?

Or consider any of our opinions. We hold them because we know we're right. We also believe that any reasonable person would share our views. How could they *not*? Social scientist David Myers' textbook *Social Psychology, Fifth Edition* offers us the results of several studies that support the Lake Wobegon Effect thesis. For example, he writes that 90 percent of business managers rated their performance "above average." Harry Beckwith says as much in his 1997 edition of *Selling the Invisible: A Field Guide to Modern Marketing*. Eighty percent of workers in another study asserted they were "above average," while only 1 percent rated themselves "below average." Sixty percent of 829,000 high school seniors surveyed by the College Entrance Examination Board rated their "ability to get along with others" in the top 10 percent, while 25 percent claimed they were in the top 1 percent. None said they were "below average."

This is all very pertinent to our concerns in this book, since a 2005 American Customer Satisfaction Index (ACSI) shows that customer service in the United States is at an all-time low. How can so many people be above-average while service levels continue to drop? It's because we're legends in our own minds. In the minds of our customers we're not nearly there yet. We can't all be so wonderful when the rest of the world perceives us as not being good enough. The truth is, we're nowhere near perfect, especially in the minds and opinions of our customers, no matter how good we think we are. After all, we're human beings. We *can't* be perfect. We can be excellent, but never, ever perfect.

YEAH, YOU'RE GOOD, BUT NOT *THAT* GOOD!

I've been using the word "we," but now, at the risk of offending you, dear reader, let me make myself as clear as day: *You* are not as good as you think you are—in every sense of the word. Nobody wants to hear this. I don't even like writing the words. No one wants to be brought down to reality, and most of us don't like being the ones to do it, either. But the sooner we face up to the facts, the better able we will be at improving our brands. I am reminded of an anecdote I heard about former world heavyweight champion, Muhammad Ali. Apparently, he was on an airplane that was about to take off and he didn't have his seat belt on. A flight attendant said, "Sir, please buckle up." He looked at her with that steely gaze of his and said, "Superman don't need no seat belt." The flight attendant, steely-eyed her-

110

self, responded, "Really? Well, Superman don't need no airplane, either."

Perhaps we're hardwired through evolution to believe in our own importance. After all, it is a great instinct, perhaps a far more sophisticated version of the survival instinct most living things seem to have. Think, for example, about your own death. Yes, you can think the words, but can you actually *conceive* of the end of your existence as a human being? We simply can't do it; it's as if we're built to believe we're immortal. I believe it was Fred DeCordova, longtime friend and manager of the great comedian George Burns—who died at age one hundred— who said that Burns literally thought he was never going to die. If you know a loved one is dying, you may prepare yourself and intellectually understand that the end of life is imminent, but the impact on you emotionally cannot be understood before it happens, perhaps because there's a part of you that simply does not believe it. And that may not be such a bad thing, after all. But it can go awry.

Each of us has known someone who thought himself or herself remarkably attractive (and they weren't), remarkably talented (and they weren't), or remarkably good at something or other, say, singing (and they weren't). The sad thing about these obnoxious people is that their inflated view of themselves blinds them to improvement. They're so busy thinking they're great that they don't stop to consider what they could do better. They are the flip side of the otherwise helpful instinct to believe in our own excellence. Imagine those same people in business!

As Harry Beckwith states in his book *Selling the Invisible,* which I am expanding on, I'm not saying your brand is poor. I'm not saying your service is poor. What I am saying is that it's a wise move to *think* it's poor. It can't hurt, that's for sure. Remember, the path to creating a unique, sustainable brand is to create the ultimate customer experience, to create evangelists. If you consider your level of service poor, you'll be far more inclined to make it better than you would if you simply sat back and basked in the self-satisfaction that you're good. If we think we're better than we are, and our service is better than it is, we cannot possibly give the customer what he or she would love and what they truly deserve. If that customer is willing to spend even one minute of their valuable time and one dollar of their hard-earned money on you, then they deserve an exceptional experience. They're not obligated to spend with you, and they'll never get that time or money back. So you'd better make sure it's an incredible experience.

Of course, you should be realistic about your talents, skills, and accomplishments. You certainly don't want to sell yourself or your brand short. At the same time, however, you don't want to *overestimate* yourself or your brand. If you do, you'll eventually find out the truth of the matter, and typically in a way that is a humiliating bubble burster. More importantly, however, when you have an inflated self-image, your focus is on yourself rather than on your customer. It's a form of narcissism that is deadly for business. Recall Narcissus, the beautiful youth who fell in love with his own reflection and, consumed by it, died because his love could not be consummated. The perpetual inward turning of self-love is doomed.

AVOIDING THE LAKE WOBEGON EFFECT

There are several ways to avoid the Lake Wobegon Effect.

1. Always keep part of your gaze directed outward. If you walk in your customers' and employees' shoes, as I advise in Chapter 5, your thinking will be focused on *their* needs. The result of that orientation will be success for your brand.
2. Always be ready to reevaluate your brand. Constantly ask yourself how you can improve upon the experience you offer your customers.
3. Focus not only on what's working, but find the aspects of your brand that are not succeeding.

The successful brands we've seen so far, from individuals like Oprah Winfrey to companies like Costco, all implicitly or explicitly understand the Lake Wobegon Effect and how to avoid it. These, however, are often the exception. The majority fail to see the importance of getting over themselves, and fall prey to the fallacy of thinking they're better than they are.

Carrier is an excellent case study of the sort of company that thinks it's better than it really is. As you know, my agency worked for Carrier. In one meeting in Indianapolis with the director of Global Marketing and other management personnel, I advised them to treat their dealers better, as the ultimate customers. "Look, the reason you're starting to lose ground is because you're forgetting who your customers are. They aren't the homeowners; your customers are the dealers, the installers, the guys who are buying from you, and then turning around and recommending your brand and installing it in homes. If you don't make these guys happy, if you don't figure out a way to support them, to help them grow their business, you're not going to get into the homes."

The Global Marketing director responded sharply, "The homeowners want our blue oval. They want Carrier. If the dealer doesn't want to do what we tell them to do, we'll find a different dealer, because the customer is asking for Carrier by name."

"No, they're not. They're asking the dealer what *he* recommends, and *that's* what's getting installed. Once the dealer stops recommending Carrier, they won't be installed in the homes."

It should come as no surprise that Carrier's brand has not retained the luster it once enjoyed. When I later saw the film *A Few Good Men*, I was reminded of that director's attitude. Recall the Jack Nicholson character, Colonel Jessup, who presumptuously and contemptuously says in response to Tom Cruise's character's demand for the truth:

You can't handle the truth! Son, we live in a world that has walls, and those walls have to be guarded by men with guns. Who's gonna do it? You? . . . I have a greater responsibility than you can possibly fathom. You don't want the truth because deep down in places you don't talk about at parties, you want me on that wall! You need me on that wall! I have neither the time nor the inclination to explain myself to a man who rises and sleeps under the blanket of the very freedom that I provide, and then questions the manner in which I provide it! I would rather you just said, "Thank-you," and went on your way.

AVOIDING THE LAKE WOBEGON EFFECT

One of the reasons we reviled Nicholson's character in the film is because he oversteps his bounds. He goes from protector to murderer and believes himself justified. The Carrier company's attitude toward their customers—and, frankly, toward my agency—was one of superiority, and it wasn't justified.

Carrier, of course, is not the only company that got too big for its britches. In 2006, Time Warner bought out Comcast Cable. A series of commercials airing in Los Angeles, one of the cities affected by the change, assured customers that the transition would be seamless; Comcast customers wouldn't even realize their cable or Internet service provider had changed. The implication was that service was terrific to begin with and would continue to be so under Time Warner's ownership and management. Unfortunately, this turned out to be entirely untrue for at least one customer in Southern California who disappeared into the new call center maze, never to be heard from again. Well, that last part's not entirely true, but you get the idea. A simple wireless router issue turned into about eight hours of phone calls, at least three technician visits, unfulfilled promises to return calls, and all around incompetence.

Dealing with large corporations often gives customers the feeling that they're in some sort of surreal universe in which one gets lost in a maze of disconnected departments. With each call transfer, the customer must retell his tale of woe anew— even after the previous representative assures said customer that the details of *their* call have been duly logged. Soon enough, the customer feels increasingly like Odysseus must have felt in his 10-year epic struggle to reach home. (Will this call be the one that finally resolves my problem?)

Not only that, but the customer is frequently told one thing by one so-called customer service representative, only to be told by another that the information was incorrect. Then, the caller is told that the company does not stand by the initial, "incorrect" information. Clearly, many companies do not think continuity or accountability is important, and the customer quickly realizes that the company's proverbial left hand has no idea what the right hand is doing. Departments are neither physically nor systematically integrated. Worse yet, many large companies seem to have set up their call centers to specifically *avoid* allowing customers to reach real people. Still, they believe their brand can withstand a model that breaks their brand promise, thereby generating negative customer word of mouth—what I've called antievangelism. This belief is either naïve or remarkably cynical.

There are people thinking about the outsized britches problem in one way or another. Former Microsoft COO Bob Herbold, for example, claims in his *Fiefdom Syndrome* that people who have been in the same job for several years are legacy people who, because they want to protect the products or services they helped create, are unlikely to be innovative. Accordingly, people create fiefdoms in which they consolidate power within their company. The results can be disastrous. In an interview with the technology business magazine *Information Week*, Herbold said that having an inflated sense of self-worth "is how they go to sleep at night." Thinking you're better than you are "is the sort of thing that can cause entire companies to go down. . . . You're blocked from being sufficiently paranoid to what might be around the corner." Now,

I'm not advocating you go around in a state of paranoia, but a healthy level of open-mindedness is essential to lasting brand success.

We mistakenly think that brands are established and then fixed when we think of brands as simply messages, logos, or objects. Instead, when we alter our perspective to think of brands in terms of personal relationships, we begin to see that brands are dynamic entities.

CHAPTER 7

YOU TALKIN' TO ME?

You Never Know Who You're Dealing With!

"PUSS-IN-BOOTS"

Once upon a time, there was an old miller who had three sons. He owned a successful mill and could not leave the mill upon his death to all three of them. But since he also had a donkey and a cat, he decided there was enough for each son to have. When the miller died, he left his mill to his oldest son, his donkey to his middle son, and the cat to his youngest son.

The eldest son was delighted, since the mill was already successful, and his father had trained him well to run it. The second son was pleased to have the donkey, since the creature could pull a cart and help till the fields on the son's farm. The youngest son was not at all excited about his inheritance. "What will I do with a cat?" the poor son wondered, utterly destitute.

Looking confidently up at the young man the cat said, "Don't worry. I can help you." "What? *You?*" the young man cried in disbelief.

"Yes," replied the cat. "It's true. Just wait. I have a plan already." With no other options, the youngest son could do nothing but wait and see what would happen. Besides, he liked the small creature. It was sleek and sprightly, and liked to curl up with him near the fire while he read at night.

Pleased to try to help his new master, the cat got dressed up in a fine velvet cape, a large felt cap with a beautiful peacock feather tucked in the side, and tall, gleaming leather boots. "Wait here," said the cat. "I'll return later."

The cat trotted away into the forest where he caught a meaty rabbit. He brought it to the king and told him it was from a wealthy marquis. Removing his hat and bowing deeply, the cat said, "Your Royal Highness, the eminent marquis has humbly sent to you this fine hare." Duly impressed, the king accepted the rabbit. Then the cat returned to his master.

Every day, the cat brought the king a present, until the king decided he wanted to meet this mysterious, generous, and sophisticated marquis. "Inform the marquis I shall make my appearance at his castle on the morrow."

The cat was delighted and raced home to tell his master, who was himself far from pleased. "But I'm poor!" the youngest son cried. "The king will have my head the moment he sees me! I'll never convince him I am the eminent marquis."

"Don't worry," the cat said, licking his paw. "I'll take care of it."

The next morning, the king and his entourage began their journey to visit the marquis. Just ahead of the king and his entourage was the cat and his master. The cat, once again dressed in his finery, had asked his master to follow him to the river, whereupon he pushed the young man in. "What! What! What have you done!" stammered the aggrieved, and now cold, young man. "I have no other clothes, and now these are soaked!"

"Don't worry," assured the cat. "I'll take care of it. Just call out to the king and his entourage when they pass by. Tell him you were out for a stroll and fell into the river." Then the cat raced away.

Nearby was a mean old ogre's castle. The ogre was horrible to all the peasants in the village and just as mean to cats. The cat pounded on the door of the ogre's castle. "What do you want?" the ogre demanded. "Tell me and then I will eat you."

The cat smiled up at him and said, "I've heard you can turn yourself into an elephant."

Not one to be bashful, the ogre agreed. "Indeed," he said.

"But," continued the cat, holding his paws apart about two inches. "I am sure you're not powerful enough to turn yourself into a tiny little mouse."

The ogre huffed and sniffed. "I can so!" the ogre cried and promptly became a mouse.

At that very moment, the cat pounced on the ogre—now mouse—and ate him. Meanwhile, the king had found the young man and had his entourage fish him out of the river. Then the king commanded his entourage to get the young man new clothes befitting a marquis' stature. Then, they all went on together to the marquis' (new!) castle.

The moral of the story: Understand the "reach of influence" of the people you deal with and how to take advantage of it.

YOUR ACTIONS GENERATE FAR-REACHING RIPPLES

You never know who you're dealing with, and you never know how far is the reach of your actions. Think about throwing a rock into water. Ripples radiate out in all directions, the result of the weight pushing the water down, and then the water rising back up to its equilibrium point again. Even after the water at the point where the rock was dropped returns to equilibrium, ripples continue. There's not just one ripple from the displacement of water caused by the one rock. Instead, there are multiple ripples, and those ripples travel very far.

Human actions also create a ripple effect. People perceive actions in certain ways and respond to those perceptions accordingly. In terms of human actions, then, I would rephrase the ripple notion this way: Profound, lasting effects can come from small, seemingly insignificant actions. Every day, we perform hundreds, if not thousands, of actions. We yawn, we smile, we walk, we sit down. Most of our actions and interactions are typically uneventful; in the span of human events, they're arguably insignificant. A handshake here, a kind word there. These things don't seem to be of enormous importance in our lives or in the course of human history. As a result, we often forget that they are, nevertheless, meaningful, or what's worse, we choose altogether to refuse to exchange pleasantries or engage in small acts of human kindness.

SOME WORDS ARE ACTIONS

This attitude toward your actions can be disastrous for you personally and for your organization or business. You could, from one small act, create either a major antievangelist or a major evangelist for your business. How often have you broken a promise to another person?

"I promise to call you back in five minutes."

"I promise to have this package sent out today."

"I promise to fix the problem."

"I promise this won't happen again."

You might think that breaking promises isn't a big deal. So what if a phone call doesn't get returned when you said it would? Is it such a big deal if you miss the shipping deadline for the day? Does it really matter if I don't fix the problem—can't someone else do it? It *is a big deal! It* does matter! Why? Because our verbal and written commitments are actions. In other words, when we say, "I promise," we are thereby *doing.* Making a promise is an *act* of speech. To promise is to perform an act. That is precisely what's involved in the making. The doing is in the saying! Consider an official who pronounces two people married. The act is the pronouncement.

Part of the reason we place such importance on making promises is precisely because they are actions, and actions result in consequences. Actions are like rocks tossed into the water; they create ripples. Consider the following types of promises, and how important these are to us as beliefs that guide and shape our lives:

- Two people getting married make vows to each other: "I promise to have and to hold . . ."
- A person utters an oath of allegiance: "I pledge allegiance to the flag . . ."
- A person takes an oath of office: "I solemnly affirm . . ."
- A witness swears to tell the truth exclusively and completely: "I swear . . ."

These are significant promises, but so are business and personal promises to keep appointments, to call people back, and so forth. Some of the very acts we often think are insignificant are, in fact, profoundly important. Why? Because they are all the same insofar as they are all *doing* the same thing, namely *making* promises! And when you do something, it affects other people.

I've been talking a lot in this book about creating unique, emotional, one-of-a-kind experiences for your customers. I'm not talking about Las Vegas-style, over the top productions. I'm not talking about lavish events. I'm talking about connecting with people in a way that truly expresses your acknowledgment and understanding of their needs. I'm talking about creating a brand whose promise is understood as an *act* that creates a far-reaching, positive ripple effect in the form of evangelists who are ready to sing your praises and bring others to you for the same experiences they had. When that promise is broken, on the other hand, the negative ripple effect creates the *anti*evangelist.

AVOIDING NEGATIVE RIPPLES

The problem is that many individuals simply don't consider their reach of influence; they don't consider the ways in which brand promises are broken. According to an article published on the University of Pennsylvania's Wharton School of Business web site, a dissatisfied customer is very likely to talk about their negative experiences with friends, but less likely to express their dissatisfaction directly to the business. The article cites the results of The Retail Customer Dissatisfaction Study

2006, which was conducted by the Verde Group and the Baker Retailing Initiative at Wharton. The statistics are interesting. One out of every three dissatisfied customers complain to an average of four people they know. Moreover, these four people then avoid the store in question based solely on the negative word of mouth. When customers have a negative experience, "only 6% of shoppers who experienced a problem with a retailer contacted the company, but 31% went on to tell friends, family, or colleagues what happened. Of those, 8% told one person, another 8% told two people, but 6% told six or more people." As Wharton marketing professor Stephen J. Hoch tells us, "Even though these shoppers don't share their pain with the store, they do share their pain with other people, apparently quite a few other people." Thus, negative word of mouth is more damaging to a business than is a direct negative experience.

Interestingly enough, a sort of telephone game phenomenon occurs when people start talking about their negative experiences. As the stories spread, people who are not directly involved in the experience hear embellished versions of the actual event. With antievangelism the ripples don't get smaller as they move out away from the origin of the story; they get bigger! "Almost half those surveyed, 48%, reported they have avoided a store in the past because of someone else's negative experience." Contrast that with the percentage of people who actually had the negative experience and reported they would not likely return to shop at the location again: 33 percent! These are numbers *everyone* should consider each and every time they have the opportunity to create a positively memorable experience.

It's especially important, given the fact that you typically won't have any idea that you've created an antievangelist. That's because you count on your customers to report their negative experiences to you. And the fact is, they don't. The researchers in the Wharton study concluded that most customers feel resigned to similar experiences in the future and simply don't think it's worth it to complain to the business in question. (Though men are more likely than women to complain, the gender differences in this regard are negligible.) Besides, when customers have multiple negative experiences with a variety of businesses, they report that they just don't have the time or energy to note every negative instance. "Indeed, the survey showed that 46% of those who had a problem expect they would definitely or probably experience the same problem in the future."

I like to think of the following case study as paradigmatic of how to create an antievangelist. Don't forget the Ben & Jerry's case study in Chapter 2, in which we learned that turning a customer into an evangelist is a crucial way to build your business. Evangelists are created by brands that overdeliver on the promises they make, brands that continually create unique experiences for their customers. An antievangelist, on the other hand, is created by either a uniquely *negative* experience, so that the customer develops a negative belief about the brand, or by simply maintaining the status quo service. The story I'm about to tell you is, in fact, something of a combination of both these elements that create antievangelists—and it happened to me. I made a brief reference to it in Chapter 1, but now I'm going to give you the whole story.

For nearly 20 years, my wife and I were loyal card-carrying

Sears customers. We have the purchases to prove it. Everything in our house is Sears, from the appliances like the dishwasher and microwave, to landscaping tools like weed-whackers, the push-mower, and the rider-mower. In short, we were a Sears household!

Several years ago Sears' service level began to fall. We weren't happy, but we were also not *un*happy enough to start shopping at another store for the same stuff—that is, until a couple of years ago when we bought a brand new washer and dryer. Within five months a little switch that engages the spin cycle on the washer broke. So I called Sears service and requested a service call. It started out well. The customer service representative said, "Sir, that's a $12 part. You don't want to pay $150 for a service call for a $12 part, do you?"

I told her I appreciated the heads up, but even if I just bought the part, I wouldn't know how to access the area of the machine where the part goes to replace it. There were no screws anywhere and apparently no way to open it up to even get to the switch.

"Okay," she said. "For another $12 we'll sell you the manual. You'll have it fixed in 30 minutes. The package will be there in three days." True to her word, three days later the package showed up. Again, so far, so good. The Sears brand was intact.

I called my father-in-law, John, to come over and help. He's a handyman. I am not. We unplugged the washer, unhooked the hoses, pulled the washer out of the cabinet, tipped it on its front, put some towels down to soak up the water running out, and then I opened the package—only to find the part was there, but not the manual! Even my handyman father-in-law couldn't figure out how to get into this machine. So I went downstairs and called Sears' parts department. This is where things went downhill fast, at practically breakneck speed.

The young lady who answered the phone was, as I like to refer to her, The Valley Girl. Gum snapping and attitude toting, this girl did everything, and I mean *everything* in her power to *not* help me! I told her the package showed up, but there was no manual. She said, "Okay, I see that's on back order? You should have it in five to seven days."

"No," I responded. "That's not going to work. I have an angry wife, a pile of clothes on the floor waiting to be washed, a father-in-law standing here ready to replace the part, there's water leaking all over the floor. I need the information now. I already paid for it, so I should have it."

There was silence on the other end.

"I'll tell you what," I continued. "Here's my e-mail address. E-mail the instructions to me."

She responded with a vague question–statement, "Um, we don't have the instructions in that format."

I said, "Okay, then go get a manual and fax the pages. Here's my fax number."

"Uh, I don't have access to the manuals," she said in a tone of voice that indicated it should be obvious to me that she wouldn't have access to the manuals.

Trying to be patient, I asked, "What do you mean you don't have access to the manuals?" After all I had called a parts department. One would think that there would be manuals all over the place.

Maybe there were, but all she said was, "I can't find them." I asked to speak to her manager, and she said, "He's off today."

Now it was time to take a different tack. I knew I would get nowhere with Miss Valley Girl, so I said as calmly as I could, "Okay then, get me the phone number to one of your service people—*any* service person. I don't care where they are. I just want to know where the bloody screws are so I can get into the washer!"

Ever unhelpful, and obviously irritated that I wouldn't just go away, Valley Girl snapped, "We don't *have* phone numbers to our service people."

"What?!" I was incredulous and at the same time irritated myself that I was stuck with someone who refused to help in any way. "How," I asked, "do you get them out on a service call?"

As you can imagine by now, her response was a dead end. "That's another manager."

Taking a deep breath, I said, "Then get me that manager."

"Oh," she said in a tone of voice that dripped the sort of ennui that only teenagers seem capable of. "She's on break."

This was the moment I became a Sears antievangelist. Sears screwed up when it sent the part without the manual. Sears screwed up by not informing me in advance or even by placing a note with the part that the manual was on back order. Sears screwed up by not doing everything in its power to deliver on the promise it made when the original customer service representative told me that I'd have the part *and* the manual within three days. Now, I was having a terrible—but perhaps all-too-common—customer service experience. I said to Valley Girl, "Well, get your manager *off* break."

The deathblow came next. "She's out of the building. I can't find her."

"Arrrggghhhhh!!!" I slammed the phone down. This service representative did everything in her power to *not* help me! She didn't know who I was and she didn't care. She just wanted me off her phone and out of her life.

So I went upstairs and told John, "We're on our own. I just got off the phone with some valley girl and we have no help." We tore the machine apart and *three hours later* had it back together again. We slid it back into the cabinet, plugged it in, hooked up the hoses, and turned it on. It worked! Thank goodness it worked.

The first thing I did after my generous father-in-law had left was take my Sears credit card out of my wallet and cut it in half. Later, when my wife got home from work I asked her for her card. "Sure," she said handing it over.

"Thanks." Then I pulled out my scissors and cut her card up, too.

"Why did you do that?" she asked. When I told her the story she said, "Good. We don't need them anymore."

We haven't set foot in a Sears store since. In a few short minutes, Sears lost two customers and nearly 20 years of loyalty. Twenty years! That's a pretty big deal, right? Sure it is, but that's not creating the ripple effect I've been discussing. You know what is? Every week I'm in front of large corporate audiences all over the country telling this story! And now my story is in this book. I've become the Sears Antievangelist!

Notice how fast a brand can be undermined with a single, profoundly negative experience. Some branding experts talk about the creation of a brand through aggregate experiences—the collected impressions of a number of experiences. But this view is incomplete. One bad experience can do more harm than several really good ones. After all, our ability to survive is connected not just to learning over time what's good for us, but more important, to learning very quickly what to avoid. That education comes in the form of pointedly negative experiences like burning one's hand in a fire. It also underscores just how crucial it is for each of your customers to have repeatedly positive experiences with you so that a strong relationship can be built—one that can withstand the occasional middling experience that results from a brand misstep.

You create brand evangelists or antievangelists by keeping and overdelivering on your brand promise, or failing to do so. Crying wolf is the surest way to create antievangelists, to turn small ripples in concentric circles into tidal waves of negative word of mouth. On the other hand, you can surf the perfect evangelical waves you generate from the trust your brand establishes. Remember from the Introduction that the most successful relationships are those built on trust. That trust is achieved through the memorable, positively one-of-a-kind experiences you create for your customers. You're able to create these for your customers not only because you continually step into their shoes, but also, as we'll see in the next chapter, because your beliefs, values, and identity are what define your brand. They are expressed through the way you truly listen to your customers and seek to transform the moment for them in positive ways they never expected. In all aspects of our lives, our actions affect other people. When we act, we are the metaphorical rocks jumping into the water and creating ripples. Your brand promise is inextricably tied to your reputation, and you want to make a big enough splash that delivering on your promise ripples indefinitely!

CHAPTER 8

Just Call Me Slick!

People Really Hate to Be "Sold"

"The Wolf in Sheep's Clothing"

A crafty wolf connived to get himself some sheep by infiltrating a flock. In his lair, he found an old sheepskin and put it on. Then he sneaked down the hill and slipped into the flock without detection. All I have to do, he thought to himself, is wait until the end of the day. Then, when the shepherd puts us in the pen for the night, I will have any sheep I want. Satisfied with his plan, he lay down and took a nap.

That evening, the wolf was herded into the pen along with the sheep. Now all I have to do is wait until the shepherd goes to sleep, and I can dine to my heart's content. But the shepherd decided he wanted some mutton on his table that night, and so before he left the pen, he reached out and laid hold of a sheep to bring back with him to his house. Sadly for the wolf, *he* was the mutton for the shepherd's dinner!

The moral of the story: You are your brand and your brand is you! Pretending to be something or someone else can be devastating.

WHAT WE'VE ACCOMPLISHED SO FAR

By now you know that branding is not exclusively about business identity in the form of a logo or advertising. You might recognize the Nike brand from its iconic swoosh logo. You might immediately think of McDonald's when you think of fast food because McDonald's commercials are ubiquitous, but by this point, you know that icons and awareness do not constitute a brand.

You also know that big businesses are not the only brands. Your business does not have to be the size of GM, Microsoft, AOL Time Warner, or Wal-Mart. Your business could be run out of your home with you as the sole employee. You could conduct business from a small office with a single assistant or in a store with several employees. The size, scope, and location of your business does not change the fact that it's a brand, nor should any of these factors truly impact your brand if you're focusing on one-on-one relationships.

Businesses are not the only brands, either. Every individual is a brand, as are organizations from nonprofits to political parties to social clubs. For example, the Gates Foundation, the Red Cross, UNICEF, Make-A-Wish Foundation, Boy Scouts, Girl Scouts, Kiwanis Clubs, Rotary Clubs, Republican Party, and Democratic Party—all are brands. The concept of branding I've been articulating is personal, which means *everyone* needs to develop one.

Each category—from individuals to organizations to businesses large and small—brings its own brand development challenges. At the same time, however, these challenges are minimized when you understand your brand identity.

Throughout this book, I have written about creating unique and memorable experiences for your customers. Chapter 2 defines a brand in terms of establishing relationships with your customers. Chapter 3 distinguishes between types of experiences you can generate for your customers, and differentiates a brand experience from ones that are merely transactional or simply meet customer expectations. Chapter 4 highlights the importance of changing your perspective to adopt your customer's point of view, rather than emphasize your product or service. Chapter 5 analyzes the results of changing your perspective. Chapter 6 admonishes you to avoid overstating your own worth. Finally, Chapter 7 focuses on the ripple effects of your actions. Thus, most of the facets of branding I've been articulating since the beginning of this book have emphasized how you affect the customer's perceptions. In other words, I've been talking about the customer's connection to your brand. Now I'm going to talk about how *you* perceive your own brand, and about *your* connection to your own brand.

CREATING AN AUTHENTIC BRAND IDENTITY: SINCERITY CAN'T BE FAKED!

First, you must take stock of your brand identity. In the Introduction to this book I state that *everyone* is a brand. Everyone has a brand identity, but not everyone understands their own brand correctly or even knows what it is. You cannot develop an authentic, sincere brand without this understanding. And you cannot create brand evangelists—people who trust you and praise your brand every chance they get—without an authentic, sincere brand. You *earn* someone's trust through your actions, so you'd better know how to act!

Understanding your brand identity, and developing the trust that turns your customers into evangelists, involves knowing what your own beliefs and values are. The fact is, when you walk in your customers' shoes, when you change your perspective to deliver the impossible, you're reflecting a core element of your identity, your values, and your beliefs. When you are sincere about trying to understand your customers' needs, desires, and what they'd truly love from you, a genuine connection is made that is the foundation of trust between you and your customers.

Compassion and sincerity can't be faked. Branding is not a matter of putting on a persona that others will like. It's not playing a role, putting on a mask, or pretending; all that is superficial, a veneer that covers up the real you. Moreover, a veneer can be quickly spotted. I don't think there's anyone that hasn't had the experience of being "sold." It's uncomfortable precisely because it's not authentic. The experience simply feels hollow. Think about the slick car salesman who's "going to do what it takes to get you into this car!" Maybe he's heavy on the hale-fellow-well-met demeanor or drenches you with flattery. When the time comes to make an offer on the car, he engages in an overly dramatic show of anxiety. "I'm gonna see my manager right now and see if I can talk him into this one. Between you and me, he's having a bad day, but I'm really gonna work on him." Eventually, the long-drawn-out ceremonial dance ends with you signing the lease or sale papers, but you walk away knowing the whole experience could have been different, and you dread the prospect of going through it again.

CREATING AN AUTHENTIC BRAND IDENTITY

Why do you dread it? What has soured you on going through the process again? In a word: insincerity. Insincerity is the wolf trotting around in sheep's clothing pretending to be something he's not. When you experience a wolf in sheep's clothing, you're soured on future interactions. It is this sort of insincerity that destroys a brand or prevents an authentic one from being established.

The car salesman example is cliché, just like the saleswoman at the clothing store who tells you every single piece of clothing you try on looks *so* good! Though they're cliché for a reason, we tend to forget just what that reason is. We instantly recognize the cliché, but not what made it true in the first place. So let me give you a personal example that should renew your grasp of how damaging insincerity can be to the branding process, and how stark the contrast is between it and an authentic brand.

My wife and I decided to remodel our kitchen. We went around to quite a few designers, showrooms, and builders. Everywhere we went, we got the same gladhanding and the same questions: "What's your budget?" "What're you looking for?" "What colors do you want to use?" "What styles interest you?" No matter what we looked at, we heard the same thing: "That's a nice look." "That's a terrific appliance." No one asked us questions about our house and how it would tie in to what we were trying to do.

Then we met Brian, a designer at MKS Kitchens. After greeting us, he started asking us about our lives. He wanted to know how many kids we have, how much we entertain, how often the kids have friends over, what sorts of foods we like to eat, what we eat most often, how much traffic we get in the kitchen and the rest of the house—how we lived and where we lived the most in our house. For 20 minutes he asked us questions and never once asked about budgets or colors or styles. During that time, he never once showed us an appliance, cabinet, or countertop. In fact, after a while, we weren't talking about kitchens at all, but our lives and how we want to improve them. The kitchen had receded far into the background because, in a way, the project wasn't about the kitchen at all. It was only one outcome of what we wanted to do in our lives at this moment.

When he did start asking about cabinets and appliances, he asked us why we had a certain cabinet color or make of appliance in mind. Later, he came to the house armed with ideas based on the conversation we'd had at his showroom. He did drawings of potential layouts and only when he had a really good idea of what we wanted did he even reference a budget. Everything he recommended was based on the conversation we had about our lives. His business sold top-of-the-line appliances, like SubZero and Wolf. But, he told us, "To be perfectly honest, I'd probably send you somewhere else for your appliances. What I sell is for people who practically live in their kitchens, people who are really into cooking and baking. You don't need, for example, a commercial grade oven."

After Brian had completed his estimate and left, I turned to my wife and said, "I want to work with him." "Why?" she asked. "Because I trust him. I like him and I trust him. It's not about cabinets and appliances; it's about *us*." I trusted Brian not simply because he knew what he was talking about and could redesign a superior kitchen for us, but because he cared about what would be best for our family.

CREATING AN AUTHENTIC BRAND IDENTITY

The profundity of this sort of authentic sincerity must not be underestimated. It reveals our deepest need to have our existence acknowledged by others. We trust someone who genuinely sees us, not an opportunity for a sale or a means to some other end. Someone who looks into our eyes and seeks to understand us is someone authentically sincere. It cannot be faked, and it is the core around which your brand is created. In other words, your identity is not sheep's clothing!

Remember that creating positive, unique experiences for others is what builds and sustains your customers' perception of your brand. Since your values and beliefs—in short, your identity—are at the heart of your brand, these are what ultimately generate the sorts of experiences your customers have. In this way, the two sides of creating and sustaining a brand—what your customer experiences and your core identity—are united. When you walk in your customers' shoes, you create a brand that reflects *your* identity, be it individual, organizational, or commercial. Unique experiences that aren't sincere won't create a sustainable brand. That's because we *know* when we're being "sold." By and large, we know when we're dealing with someone for whom we're just an opportunity for a sale. Some people may mistake the idea of walking in their customers' shoes as simply an opportunity to make a sale, but it's not sincere, and as such, it won't result in a lasting brand.

Branding is about emotional relationships, and most people are too sophisticated to be deceived by someone who only pretends. Most of us are not taken in by the car salesman's lavish displays of attention any more than we are duped by crocodile tears or deceived by a smile that looks like the person is trying too hard. You can't divest yourself of your brand. So when you try to be something you're not, it shows! You've got to be unique, a personality that truly belongs to you. Hopefully, that personality is compassionate and giving—the requirements for a sustainable brand. You've got to truly listen, truly change places with your customer, and then with sincerity, try to figure out how to transform the moment.

INAUTHENTIC BRAND IDENTITIES

Some people may mistake the idea of listening to what the customer is turned on by as a means of manipulating a sale. A lot of people have the *ability* to listen, but they are simply looking for a customer's hot buttons. They use the idea of transforming the moment as a device for creating customer excitement about a product or sale. For these people, the whole premise of listening to a customer is to exploit. Don't make these same mistakes! The sincerity that builds trust involves genuinely asking yourself what it would be like to be your customer, right now; it involves listening to what your customer says so that you can help them transform *their* lives, not yours. Evangelists *trust* your brand because they trust *you*. Think, for example, about how quickly marriages disintegrate without trust. Brand loyalty is a marriage of trust between two people.

A glaring and shocking example of how trust can be instantaneously eroded comes from a giant of charitable organizations, the American Red Cross. In the hours after terrorists attacked the United States on September 11, 2001, record-breaking pledges poured in from around the world. According to various news reports, including CBS and CNN, more than 1,000 chapters of the American Red Cross and other charitable organizations received donations that eventually exceeded *$1 billion.* The donations reflected the desperate desire of people to help, to help begin the healing after the horrific disaster. The intention was for the money to go directly to 9/11 relief. The Red Cross set up The Liberty Fund as a direct response to the attacks and collected more than $564 million. However, by November 2001, CNN and other news agencies reported that only $154 million of that had been distributed. According to a CBS news article, "a dozen of the Red Cross chapters audited were marking, or "coding," donations as local funds. This means chapters like San Diego, Southwest Florida, and Gateway Area, Iowa, would keep the money instead of sending it in for Sept. 11 victims. Worse yet, accountability was apparently lax. Chapters of the Red Cross were operating in some instances independent of the central organization, and some did not have accurate accounts of the funds they had received post-9/11. Dr. Bernadine Healy, who was the outgoing Red Cross president at the time, argued in defense of the charitable organization's decision to set aside more than half of the money raised for future needs, including possible terrorist attacks. That's where the Red Cross brand failed.

The Red Cross' planning may have been wise, but apparently they grossly misunderstood their customer—in this case, the donors. Donors believed their money was going directly to 9/11 assistance. The fact that a lot of donor money was being set aside meant to many that their money was not reaching the intended recipients. In other words, though donors were not critical of the charity having money for future disasters, the real question was whether the important agency *misled* donors into thinking that donations were going immediately to 9/11 relief—everything from blood donations to assisting rescue workers and victims' families. People had mortgages to pay, overwhelming medical bills, and jobs lost; the practical effects of the mass murders were as widespread as the psychological impact was deep.

What people needed most was to know that charitable organizations would help those who needed it and help them right away. In large measure, the help was immediate. Unfortunately, however, of those charities that collected donations, the Red Cross in particular went into corporate organization mode. In the process, it seems as if it forgot about its brand. During a hearing in November 2001 in front of the House Energy and Commerce Committee's oversight panel, Dr. Healy said, "The Liberty Fund is a war fund. It has evolved into a war fund," she said. "We must have blood readiness. We must have the ability to help our troops if we go into a ground war. We must have the ability to help the victims of tomorrow." For donors, this wasn't the point!

I don't think anyone really believes the Red Cross deceived people for some selfish, greedy end. The organization has a long history of good works. But in a moment when individuals' feelings were of raw helplessness and despair, and the only way they had to connect with and help others was through monetary donations, the Red Cross failed to keep its brand trust. Indeed, if the reports are to be believed, the charitable agency deceived donors into thinking their money was helping in a way it wasn't—even though it would go to help someone, somewhere, at some point.

The Red Cross example illustrates not only the fact that trust can be eroded, but also the fact that not all instances of lost trust are due to false pretenses. The fact is, some people who fail to build a successful brand are not trying to be deceptive. Instead, they may simply not know what their brand is, or they may misunderstand it. Suppose our car salesman—let's call him Slick—is not attempting to put on a false show of sincerity but simply does not understand his brand. It's not that they're trying to be deceitful; it's not that they're trying to be insincere. It's just that they don't have an identity or they have a mistaken idea of what their identity should be. Slick believes that sales are about glad handing and flattery; it's a big show. Perhaps he got into sales because he was an outgoing, popular guy in high school. He was funny, the class clown. People wanted to be around him because he was enthusiastic and funny. Let's further assume that these behaviors became part of Slick's persona, an assumed identity that did not really reflect who he was, perhaps because he never really considered who he was and what his values were. Slick had unwittingly created an image based on the positive responses he had received in school, and the real person underneath was never developed further.

When Slick went into sales, he simply projected this popular-guy persona. As a result of the created image, as a result of working through an identity that wasn't himself, he comes off as insincere at best, or smarmy at worst. Brands aren't about shtick or superficial persona; they're about the experiences created by the sincere expression of one's identity. This is constituted largely by one's values and belief system—the sort of things we learned from the children's stories our parents read to us when we were little!

In Chapter 1, I talk about individual brands like presidents Clinton and G.W. Bush. Political discussions evoke tremendous passions from people who are loyal to a particular leader. These leaders develop their individual brands through their actions, message, and character. Their brands also have to be strong enough to overcome the negative messages and political attacks of their adversaries. The former take time to build, the latter take just seconds. Moreover, most of us don't have the opportunity to engage personally with national politicians. And yet I have advanced the idea that a successful, sustainable brand is built on unique, memorable, and personal experiences. So how can an individual who does not interact personally with a politician have such experiences? Aren't the experiences limited to what is seen on television, heard about on the radio, or read in print or online? In a word, no. The politician's message is advertised through these media, but it is their policies that connect them with voters. These policies are the tangible results of the politician's message. Implemented policies are to politicians what customer service is to a business. In turn, policies reflect a public servant's personal identity; they speak to the individual's values and beliefs.

YOUR BRAND IDENTITY IS DEEPLY PERSONAL

The same is true for *any* individual. Your own policies are your version of customer service. In short, your brand is your character, your values, your beliefs, your personal identity. And these determine the kinds of experiences people will have when they interact with you.

Jason Miller is a perfect example of a successful individual brand. He works in the Syracuse, New York, offices of Countrywide Home Loans. Year after year, he is one of the top sellers in the nation, but he works in one of the most economically depressed regions of the country. He does not only arrange multimillion dollar loans. In fact, he was recently working all day on a $32,500 loan for an African immigrant who was seeking to buy a foreclosure property for his family. This man had been working at a $10 an hour job for only six months, and only recently opened up a bank account. Before that, he had earned money under the table at a gas station. Needless to say, he has little cash, and the loan is not going to make Jason—who, like other loan officers, works on commission only—a lot of money. But Jason spent *hours* on the phone trying to secure a loan for this man. Why? Two related reasons: He knows how important this loan is for the man—getting a house means *the world* to him—and Jason genuinely wants to help, and he's got the expertise to do it.

Let's analyze further this notion of something meaning the world to somebody. We seem to think that we should create service levels similar to a hierarchy according to the amount of money people spend. So you get amazing service at a Five Star restaurant because you're blowing $500 on a meal for two, or you're treated like royalty because you're buying the high-end luxury car. However, as the price goes down, so does the service level. The correlation between service and price reflects a complete *lack* of understanding what a brand is. If you can't afford a $500 meal, does this mean you deserve to be treated poorly? No! If you can't afford a $50,000 car, does this mean you have no value as a human being? Of course not! Why? It's simple. Regardless of how much money you have, you have hopes, dreams, and aspirations. There are things you want to do and have, and these things are *meaningful* to you. It doesn't matter if they're meaningful to anyone else, but once another person knows that something means the world to you, it *should* matter.

The 1957 courtroom drama *12 Angry Men* illustrates this point. In the film based on the stage play of the same name, an eighteen-year-old boy is on trial for murdering his father. Eleven of the jurors walk into deliberations believing he's guilty. One of those jurors talks about how the boy must be guilty because he comes from a slum. There is a pervasive sense that the boy doesn't deserve consideration—despite the fact that the jurors are legally bound to undertake to do so—because he's poor. According to some of the jurors, it's as if the boy's very value as a human being is determined solely by his socioeconomic condition. Fortunately for him, one juror, played by Henry Fonda, refuses to participate in a knee-jerk vote of guilty, and his commitment to examining the evidence is the heart of the drama. Surely the outcome of the jurors' deliberations means the world to the boy!

A true brand is not going to distinguish an individual based on money. If someone like Countrywide's Jason can spend time on a $32,500 loan, it's clear that his interest is not about how much that potential buyer is spending. Instead, it's about treating that person with dignity. It's about acknowledging the fact that this individual is spending money—not how much he's spending.

People like Jason aren't punching the clock when they arrive at work. They're not thinking exclusively of sales goals. They truly understand what helping another person means, what that person is trying to accomplish, and how significant the experience is to that person. People like Jason exemplify sincerity, compassion, and generosity. They have authentically developed the skill of walking in their customers' shoes.

Such sincerity reminds me of a discussion I heard years ago on a radio program. A child psychologist highlighted a mistake parents often make when interacting with their children. He talked about a scenario in which a child, maybe age eight, comes home from school and says, "I lost my stuffed animal today," or "I lost my backpack," or "Someone was mean to me." The parent responds, "Oh, that's okay. We'll get you another one," or "We can get you another backpack, but I hope you didn't have anything important inside!" or "Don't listen to mean kids. They don't know what they're talking about." The mistake is failing to connect with the trauma the child has just experienced. Worse yet, the response essentially dismisses the child's feelings. The psychologist explained that parents who respond in this way are not actively trying to exacerbate or disregard their child's pain. It's just that they're so busy and have such enormous problems in their own adult lives that the child's problem seems trivial. Of course, to the child, the event *is* a big deal—a really big deal. It's caused them overwhelming stress. Failing to recognize and act on that recognition is effectively a failure of compassion.

When Jason looked at a $32,500 loan while one in the hundreds of thousands was sitting on his desk, he could have just passed it by. After all, the commission on $32,500 is significantly less than one on 10 times more. But Jason took on the loan; he didn't pass it on to someone else. He didn't trivialize how important having a house was to the man. He knew that, most likely, if the man could afford a six-figure home, he would buy one, but this $32,500 house is all he could afford, and it means the world to him. That, in a nutshell, is why some people are sincere, are authentic, and some aren't. As you're building your business, interacting with customers, working with employees, don't be a wolf in sheep's clothing.

Given the deeply personal nature of brand building, it would seem that individuals and small businesses would always beat out even global corporations in achieving brand loyalty and attaining financial success. But instead, it might seem more like a fantasy than a realistic business idea. After all, for example, hasn't Wal-Mart effectively crushed small retail businesses in virtually every city and town it's come to dominate? But in my definition of branding, the Wal-Mart brand cannot be sustained. Just because a company's brand is ubiquitous does not make it unconquerable. In fact, it is the very largeness of a major corporation that is its Achilles heel. Small businesses are able to be flexible in a way that large companies simply can't. Large companies are not lithe; they simply cannot turn on a dime the way a small business can. Because the intimacy between customer and small business brand is more quickly established than that between customer and large business brand, the small one can more rapidly step into the customers' shoes and deliver an amazing experience. Don't forget, branding doesn't require you to throw a lot of money into advertising; it requires the least expensive but most valuable asset of all: you.

HOW BIG ORGANIZATIONS MUST GENERATE *PERSONAL* BRANDS

You might think that making connections with other human beings seems not only obvious at the individual and small business level, it's also impossible to avoid. It's easier, on the other hand, to become isolated when large companies are involved. Most interactions take place over the Internet or on the phone, where the systems in place seem designed to keep you from actually connecting with another human being. If you do make it into a brick-and-mortar, you often deal with anonymous associates or customer service clones. There's nothing personal about the experience; it's entirely transactional. But, just because face-to-face contact, or repeated phone or e-mail contact with the same person is easier between individuals in small business and nonbusiness situations, this does not mean that emotional connections can't be established in large companies, too. Throughout this book you've read about people like Verizon's Michelene and Super 8 Motel's Nayan Patel, people who are employees or franchise owners of mind-bogglingly large corporations. But they are not mindless, featureless automatons. They are individuals engaged in their work in such a way that through their work *they* define the Verizon or Super 8 brand! On the other side of the equation are the two young women I mention in previous chapters who worked for McDonald's and Sears respectively. These large companies have become *so* large that they cannot guarantee their brands. The McDonald's cashier at LaGuardia Airport who treated everyone as if they were intrusions on her life, and the Sears customer service representative who did everything she could to avoid helping me are examples of how large companies' brands are undermined by negative customer experiences.

There are several reasons why people like Michelene are the rare exception in a large company, rather than the rule. First, corporate culture fosters in employees the sense that they don't matter, that they're easily expendable, and that they lack the power to act on behalf of the company. They quickly become entrenched in the culture because they know they're one of 30,000 employees who is paid little per hour. When the corporate attitude speaks, it says, "Just do your job and you won't get fired." Naturally, employees begin to think this way. They want to protect their little corner of the world, and if that means being unhelpful to a customer or two, so be it. After all, the company has thousands, so "you can't waste time going out of your way for one or two of them."

Usually, there's not much a single customer can do to combat this pervasive negative attitude. In fact, most customers of large corporations feel powerless to effect any sort of change. Two recent examples, however, show that the corporate attitude that filters down to employees *can* have negative consequences. One AOL (America Online) customer, Vincent Ferrari, wanted to cancel his service. Knowing the company's reputation for making cancellations difficult, Ferrari decided to tape the call. What followed—after he had waited 15 minutes for a live person—was an unbelievable exchange between the customer and the retention expert. Here is just a portion of the transcript of the call that took 20 minutes:

AOL REPRESENTATIVE: Hi, this is John at AOL. How may I help you today?

VINCENT FERRARI: I wanted to cancel my account.

AOL: Sorry to hear that. Let's pull your account up here real quick. Can I have your name please?

VINCENT: Vincent Ferrari.

AOL: You've had this account for a long time.

VINCENT: Yup.

AOL: Use this quite a bit. What was the cause of wanting to turn this off today?

VINCENT: I just don't use it anymore.

AOL: Do you have a high-speed connection, like the DSL or cable?

VINCENT: Yup.

AOL: How long have you had that . . .

VINCENT: Years. . . .

AOL: The high speed?

VINCENT: Years.

AOL: Well, actually I'm showing a lot of usage on this account.

VINCENT: Yeah, a long time, a long time ago, not recently.

AOL: Okay, I mean is there a problem with the software itself?

VINCENT: No. I just don't use it, I don't need it, I don't want it. I just don't need it anymore.

AOL: Okay. So when you use this . . . I mean, use the computer, I'm saying, is that for business or for . . . for school?

VINCENT: Dude, what difference does it make? I don't want the AOL account anymore. Can we please cancel it?

AOL: Last month was 545 hours of usage.

VINCENT: I don't know how to make this any clearer, so I'm just gonna say it one last time. Cancel the account.

AOL: Well, explain to me what's, why . . .

VINCENT: I'm not explaining anything to you. Cancel the account.

AOL: Well, what's the matter, man? We're just, I'm just trying to help here.

VINCENT: You're not helping me. You're helping me . . .

151

AOL: I am trying to help.

VINCENT: Helping . . . listen, I called to cancel the account. Helping me would be canceling the account. Please help me and cancel the account.

AOL: No, it wouldn't actually . . .

VINCENT: Cancel my account.

AOL: Turning off your account . . .

VINCENT: Cancel the account.

AOL: . . . would be the worst thing that . . .

VINCENT: . . . . Cancel the account.

AOL: Okay, 'cause I'm just trying to figure out . . .

VINCENT: Cancel the account. I don't know how to make this any clearer for you. Cancel the account. When I say cancel the account, I don't mean help me figure out how to keep it, I mean cancel the account.

AOL: Well, I'm sorry, I don't know what anybody's done to you Vincent because all I'm . . .

VINCENT: Will you please cancel the account.

AOL: Alright, some day when you calmed down you're gonna realize that all I was trying to do was help you . . . and it was actually in your best interest to listen to me.

VINCENT: Wonderful. Okay.

Ferrari finally was able to cancel his account but posted the conversation on a web site: http://media.putfil.com/ AOL-Cancellation. When the story took off across the Internet and was picked up by various news outlets, AOL fired the representative and apologized to Ferrari. AOL also claimed it was using the tape to train its representatives *not* to behave the way "John" had, but given the widespread practice of retaining customers that led Ferrari to tape his call in the first place, AOL's contrition seems disingenuous.

A similar firing–apologizing incident took place around the same time as Ferrari's AOL debacle. This time, however, it involved cable company, Comcast. A customer posted a creatively produced video on YouTube.com showing a Comcast technician asleep on his couch. The technician was there to replace a modem when he called Comcast and was put on hold *for more than an hour!* The screen then reads, "Thanks Comcast for two broken routers, four hour appointment blocks, weeklong internet outages, long hold times, high prices, three missed appointments, for promising to call back and then not calling. Thanks Comcast for everything."

Needless to say, only *after* the video had reached a wide audience did the company take action. The technician was fired and Comcast apologized. However, there is no indication that the sort of "silo" business model that contributed to the incident has been replaced.

The "silo" business model, in which departments are isolated from each other, simply exacerbates an already problematic attitude both within the company and in terms of the brand experience. This business structure encourages employees to reflect a negative brand, and it persists until the company is forced to change, as the AOL and Comcast examples illustrate. The effects are far-reaching. Internally, co-workers are not united by a single goal; in fact, they may even do their work thousands of miles away from the nearest department. Externally, customers feel like there's no unified brand at all.

When a Time Warner customer began having Internet problems, she had a rotten experience. Her calls were transferred from one department to another. Each time, she had to repeat her story, because the previous customer service representative failed to note the salient details. Finally, she was told that a ticket would be written, and her problem referred to Home Networking. "Can't I just talk to them?" she asked. "No," was the response. "We don't have contact with them." "What do you mean, you don't have contact? Are you saying you send them messages under the door?" "We can't call them. That's why we write the ticket." "Okay, but the *last* time I called, I was told I'd need a new wireless router. Someone in your company wrote a ticket for that, and scheduled a time for a technician to come out and install it. When he came out, he had no router. There was nothing on his work order that said Router. He said he'd come back in a couple of hours, but he didn't. Someone *else* in your organization told me, 'Oh, no. We can't just send him back out. In fact, we don't have access to dispatch, so we *couldn't* just send him back out. You have to make another appointment.' So, do you see why I want to talk to the secret Home Networking department?" If ever there was a silo disconnected from other silos, this was it!

After several more minutes, the exasperated customer began to feel exactly like the child whose parent dismisses her. "Look," she said. "I'm a human being, and you're a human being. Your company has repeatedly and unrepentantly screwed up for days. I've spent hours trying to resolve your mistake, and in the process lost hours of work. I've spoken with numerous customer service representatives at who-knows-how-many call centers, and you can't—you won't—even let me speak with someone who can accept responsibility and effect change? All you can do is send messages to a man behind the curtain who sounds like the Wizard of Oz, but you can't help me. Don't you feel utterly impotent as a human being?" "Look," he said sadly. "Even if I could fix it with a phone call or e-mail, I'm here on the east coast of Canada. There's nothing *I* can do." "So you're telling me there's not one person at Time Warner who can do anything to help me right this minute? Not even anyone who can officially take responsibility in some tangible way?" "No, but I can credit you a month of Internet access." Needless to say, that call ended very shortly thereafter. The ticket typed up and sent to Home Networking was flagged Urgent.

The customer knows that the call center agent's hands are tied. It's as if large companies want it that way. Employees are hamstrung by corporate policies, and their jobs depend on following them. People like Verizon's Michelene or Countrywide's Jason just happen to be very committed to making human connections—and they're very creative about it.

Large businesses aren't as nimble as small ones, but the organizations' leaders set the tone that is translated and implemented down the line by managers and supervisors. Managers, directors, presidents—"higher-ups" on the corporate ladder—are often so far removed from the daily nourishment of their brand that values don't trickle down.

If, on the other hand, corporate leaders inspire their employees to take command and have an objective to make each individual happy, each *employee* then has the freedom to make things happen. *They* are the brand. After all, they're the ones interacting with customers of all stripes, be it buyer, distributor, reseller, and so forth. The leader of a large company can't be effective touching *every* person, but they can make sure that everyone *below* them buys into the vision and culture of the brand, and then applies it to their groups.

Employees reflect the company's values. Just ask Costco's president, Jim Sinegal. He knows that if he doesn't buy into the brand, and if he doesn't teach his team how to buy into it, then his managers won't, either, and in turn they won't inspire the feet on the ground. You don't have to compromise your values to create a successful brand—just the opposite. Ben & Jerry's owners haven't sacrificed their beliefs in order to build a brand. Instead, their beliefs *became* an essential ingredient of that brand.

You might be thinking, Sounds good, but how can I possibly get my low-wage workers to buy into my brand? Suppose you own a fast food restaurant franchise. Your employees don't get paid very much and the work is hard. Most of us think of low wage jobs as just stepping-stones to something better—a "real" career—or we think that no one who isn't desperate or un-qualified would take such jobs. The former may be true, but we'll see that this does nothing to weaken my position on sell-ing your employees on your brand. The latter is simply not true, not only because a worker's value is not identical to the money they earn. Experience disproves it.

You can inspire your employees to care—whatever their hourly wage or salary—in big and small ways. For example, in-vite employees for a cup of coffee now and then to *listen* to them talk about their work. Tell them they're important, that their job can't be done by just anybody. Tell them, "I chose *you*. You matter because you make the brand." Give your em-ployees notes thanking them for the work they do. You could even stick a Post-it note on their computer or workstation acknowledging their contributions to the brand. Just as important, be direct about their situation. There's nothing wrong with telling them that you know this job is not a career, but that it still matters how they represent the brand. After all, you never know whom you're going to meet and what opportunities will arise. Remember, a good brand creates a substantial ripple effect! As Starbucks' Howard Schultz tells us, "If people relate to the company they work for, if they form an emotional tie to it and buy into its dreams, they will pour their heart into making it better."

As the expression goes, "You're only as good as the people you surround yourself with." I add that your people are only as good as you are. Your brand expresses your identity, your beliefs, and your values. Staying true to them will make it possible for you not only to change your perspective so that you can step into your customers' shoes, but will also generate a lasting, powerful, emotional brand.

CHAPTER 9

BRANDING? LOL!

Branding for the Technology-Driven Business

"THE THREE LITTLE PIGS"

Once upon a time, there was a sow that had three little pigs. The time soon came for the little pigs to go off and seek their own fortune. "Beware of the wolf. Build yourselves strong houses, and you will be safe." With these words of advice, the sow sent them on their way.

With that, the three little pigs set off to seek their fortune. As they traveled down the road, they met a man carrying some straw. "May I have some so I can build a house?" asked the first little pig. "Yes," replied the man, "yes, you may." And he gave the first little pig enough straw to build a house.

After much work, the first little pig said, "This is a fine house. I will be safe here from the wolf."

The second little pig said, "Yes, it is a fine house. But I will make mine stronger." The third little pig said, "As will I." And they set off down the road, waving good-bye to the first little pig.

The two remaining little pigs walked for a while, and then

came upon a man carrying some sticks. "May I have some sticks so that I can build a house?" asked the second little pig. "Yes, you may," answered the man. And he gave the second little pig enough sticks to build a house.

After much work, the second little pig said, "This is a fine house. I will be safe here from the wolf."

The third little pig said, "Yes, it is a fine house. But I will make mine stronger." And he set off down the road, waving good-bye to the second little pig. The third little pig walked for a while, and then came across a man carrying a load of bricks. "May I have some so I can build a house?" The man said, "Yes, you may." And the third little pig worked all day long making his house. It was very hard work, but when he was finished, he said, "This is a fine house. The wolf cannot get me here."

The next morning, the wolf set off looking for food. When he arrived at the first little pig's house, he said sweetly, "Little pig, little pig, let me in." Upon seeing the wolf through his window, the first little pig said, "Not by the hair on my chinny-chin-chin!" This made the wolf mad. "Well, then," he said, "I shall huff and puff and blow your house in!" And that's just what he did. Then he snatched up the first little pig and gobbled him up.

The next morning, the wolf set off looking for food once again. Upon spying the second little pig's stick house, the wolf said to himself, Another choice meal will be had today! After knocking on the door, the wolf said sweetly, "Little pig, little pig, let me in." Upon seeing the wolf through his window, the second little pig said, "Not by the hair on my chinny-chin-chin!" This made the wolf mad. "Well, then," he said, "I shall huff and puff and blow your house in!" And that's just what he did. Then he snatched up the second little pig and gobbled him up.

The third morning, the wolf set off looking for food once again, this time searching for another little pig's house. He did not have to look very long before he came across the third little pig's house. Oh, how delicious this little piggie will be! he thought happily. After knocking on the door, the wolf said sweetly, "Little pig, little pig, let me in." Upon seeing the wolf through his window, the third little pig said, "Not by the hair on my chinny-chin-chin!" This made the wolf mad. "Well, then," he said, "I shall huff and puff and blow your house in!" The third little pig was very nervous but still confident about his house. He smiled and said, "Go ahead, then. Try." So the wolf drew in a huge breath and blew until his lungs were empty. But the house stood strong. The wolf tried again and again until he was exhausted. But the house stood strong. Frustrated, the wolf went away, and the third little piggy lived safely in his house thereafter.

The moral of the story: No matter what you use to build your brand, don't build it quick and easy, build it strong to make it last.

What Technology Does for Us

The tremendous growth of technology has given us remarkable means of communicating. The Age of Technology has spawned the Information Age, and with it comes terrific opportunities for your brand. What we need to learn is how to use that technology to build a successful brand in the Information Age. It is crucial to understand that *technology does not replace your brand, it enhances it.* At present, many individuals, businesses, and non-profit organizations use technology as a crutch—really an extended advertising tool that is expected to replace brand building and sustenance—rather than as a great vehicle that's only one small part of your brand-building process. Even if your business or organization exists exclusively online, technology offers continuity of brand, not the brand itself.

From the days of telegraph to telephone to cell phone; from instant messaging devices and programs like BlackBerrys, Sidekicks, and e-mail; and from faxes to the World Wide Web and Internet, people at great distances have been able to connect. Today, this connection can occur instantly, at any time, and practically from anywhere. Thus technology has benefited us in numerous ways. Forever gone are the days when messages had to be *hand delivered*, when word from friends, relatives, and business contacts could take months to reach its destination. Today, we pick up a phone and dial a number, or type a message that reaches its recipient instantly. With the click of a button we can place an order for a product or service. When emergencies arise, we're able to reach out or be contacted instantaneously. There are less urgent, but still profound, benefits of technology.

Perhaps the most revolutionary telecommunications technology today is the Internet. The computer-based global information system—which includes the World Wide Web, chat rooms, message boards, list serves, e-mail, and other communication tools—brings together people who otherwise would never meet. Never before has so much information been available at once to so many people. Everything from government documents to the latest scientific discoveries to personal Weblogs, and much more can be found. The search engines make research faster and more efficient than ever before. Whether you want to get information on various types of diets, read books online, or check out new markets for your business, the Internet is a tremendously powerful instrument.

Technological innovations in communications are, in general positive for business, both big and small. The more people with whom you can connect, the more prospects you have for establishing your brand. Once people perused print catalogs and ordered products by mail. Later, orders by phone and then fax increased the speed at which orders could be placed, and so also delivered. Now, the Internet has utterly transformed the way we shop. To take a simple example, when you browse the Internet looking for a book, you can be connected with small, independent sellers across the globe. Alibris.com, for example, is a clearinghouse for new and used books. You type in the name of the author, the title of the book, or the ISBN number, and search results list what sellers have copies of the book, its price, and the seller's description of the book. Once a purchase has been made, the seller sends you an e mail confirming shipping arrangements.

Service-based businesses also succeed online. Insurance companies, consulting firms, dating services, engineering firms, architecture firms, hospitals, wedding planners, financial advisers, business planners, nonprofit organizations—the list goes on and on. You can quickly and efficiently compare prices and benefits of various services without getting on the phone or leaving your home or office. You can scour online chat rooms for discussions of people's experiences with particular products or services. Most companies have FAQ pages on their web sites that give you information you can use to make a decision about purchasing a particular service. In fact, there is so much information online that you can find pretty much anything you seek.

THE DOWNSIDE OF MASS COMMUNICATION

But, as with most any benefit, there is a downside to the plethora of information and opportunities afforded by Internet technology. In fact, perhaps the seemingly endless list of possibilities is a little overwhelming. As a result, and despite all of these tremendous benefits, we're *so* connected to the rest of the world these days that we often feel utterly lost.

It is this phenomenon that Swarthmore College psychologist Barry Schwartz discusses in his book *The Paradox of Choice: Why More is Less*. Based on his behavioral economics and psychological research, Schwartz argues that, "unlimited choice . . . can produce genuine suffering." We humans just don't do all that well with plethora, yet technology gives us just that. Schwartz cites a study in a series by researchers at Columbia and Stanford universities entitled "When Choice is Demotivating: Can One Desire too Much of a Good Thing?" In the study, some shoppers were offered free samples from 24 jam choices, and some were offered 6. Though the greater number drew larger samples, in the end, 30 percent of those who sampled the six-jam array bought a jar, while only 3 percent of those who sampled the 24-jam array bought a jar. Schwartz offers us the results of a number of other studies, and the conclusion he draws is that we tend to be irrational in the way we measure "opportunity costs." This irrationality applies to many other aspects of our lives, from choosing a partner to choosing a career. But because of the newness of much of our technology, the shock of choice might feel more acute.

We may, then, wish to disconnect, to not be quite so available all the time or have so many choices that make it impossible to choose. We may tend to feel barraged by technology in many ways, not served by it. In the midst of all this clutter, brands have to stand out, they have to transcend the noise, the din created by the massive spread of technology into our lives.

All this might make you wonder how you could possibly connect with someone online to create an ultimate customer experience. After all, aren't there just too many choices? Isn't it impossible to stand out in the dizzying crowd? Doesn't technology isolate us, thereby eliminating the human element crucial to branding success? If we're not careful, yes. Recall the discussions in the Introduction and in Chapter 4, where we discuss how technology is hindering our ability to connect with customers and beginning to influence our own personal contact and how we communicate. If you depend on technology to the extent that it alone runs your business, then you lose all personal contact, and there's no opportunity to create emotional connections and build your brand.

Though there are numerous challenges to branding online, such as the vast and impersonal nature of the Internet, the rate of speed at which technology develops, and the aforementioned feeling of isolation generated by online interactions, technology can do wonderful things, and it doesn't have to isolate you. We will discuss how to transcend the limits of technology by using it in a creative way that is an extension of your existing brand. In so doing, you will be creating a lasting, memorable brand. So just how does branding fit into the mix of the ever-changing, unbelievably broad scope of global networks?

HOW TO USE TECHNOLOGY TO EXTEND YOUR REACH OF INFLUENCE

There are few people who have not been online. Millions of people have personal web sites, Weblogs (or blogs), and business portals. Building a brand online would seem to be a wildly daunting task. But consider brands like Amazon, MySpace, YouTube, and Google. Each is a very different type of business: (1) Amazon is an online retailer; (2) MySpace is an online meeting and marketplace for (mostly young) individuals; (3) started as a personal video sharing site in February of 2005 YouTube is, according to its About page, "a consumer media company for people to watch and share original videos world-wide through a Web experience," which means hundreds of thousands of personal (and viral marketing) videos are posted for millions and millions of people around the world to view; and (4) Google is a search engine and rapidly growing infor-mation storehouse for everything from books to videos to satellite imaging. Each of these sites connotes in their users very precise feelings, and this is no accident. In fact, Google's purchase of YouTube was made without the intention of 'google-zing' YouTube's brand, which will remain a distinct identity.

Let's consider a simple, understandable illustration of uniting the human element with technology: Apple's 2006 television ad campaign featuring two men representing a PC and a Mac. "Hello, I'm a Mac," one actor says. "I'm a PC," says the other actor. The commercial then shows how much better Macs are at a variety of things. In one commercial, PC has a cold and keeps sneezing. Mac offers him a tissue, and then asks if PC is okay. "No, I'm not okay. I have that virus that's going around. You'd better stay back. This one's a doozy." Mac says, "That's okay, I'll be fine." "No, no!" PC protests. "Do not be a hero!" He continues, his voice tense with nerves, "Last year there were a hundred and fourteen *thousand* known viruses for PCs." Mac pauses for a beat, and then shrugs off PC's worry in a slightly smug tone. "Not for Macs." Realizing his inferiority to Mac, PC says, "I gotta crash," and promptly falls over. In 30 seconds, the Apple ad has generated two *human* characters and has shown how one is healthier than the other. At the same time, the commercial simplifies technology.

This ad series is an intriguing way to humanize and simplify technology and at the same time differentiate the Mac brand PCs. Over the past 10 years or so, computers have become more and more homogenous, both in terms of their abilities to run the same programs and share hardware. At one time, for example, if you owned an Apple computer and you wanted to print a document, you could use only an Apple printer. Now, you can plug your Apple computer into virtually any brand of printer and print your document. The same goes for software and many of the physical parts of your computer. Returning to the 2006 television campaign previously mentioned, we can better see what Apple is trying to do: personalize—*humanize*—technology *and* differentiate its brand from the myriad PC brands that have flooded the market since IBM clones first emerged in the mid-1980s.

Prior to the late 1970s and early 1980s, a personal computer on one's desk was practically unthinkable to the average individual. Mainframes were used in academic and business domains exclusively, and users sat at terminals that were hooked up to the mainframes. These mainframes were enormous—often occupying an entire room—and had to be run by specially trained operators.

Fast-forward to the mid-1990s and the introduction to millions of the Internet and the World Wide Web. Never before in human history has there been an information resource on the scale of the networks known as the Internet and World Wide Web. The communication, collaboration, and information dissemination capacities alone are changing the way human beings think, interact, and work. It will be decades before the effects of this medium on the human condition are truly understood.

What we *do* understand are the elements of a successful brand. And these must be our guiding lights when we enlist technology—specifically the Internet—to help us expand and sustain our business. Let us assume you've already established a brick-and-mortar brand. For example, FedEx was a known and trusted brand long before they created a web site. Much of the brand was translated to the online version of the business, and so the brand essentially transferred seamlessly to the virtual realm. In fact, the brand improved in some ways when the business went online, as it offered its customers more ways to utilize its services.

Suppose you don't already have a known brand and you want to generate one online. You can create your brand online by adapting the very same branding techniques you use when directly connecting with your customers. Consider the questions you ask yourself when you think about your company, industry, and competitors. What do you all offer? How can you use technology to create emotional experiences, personal experiences, and not mechanistic ones? How can you make your customer's life easier when they use technology? Can you do something, for example, with your phone system that makes navigating the company easier? Can you solve a problem with technology? Can you think of at least three ways of taking the same products and services, and offering them in unique ways? Why does the world need my product or services? Why do these customers need me? How can I change my prospect's life? How can I create an unexpected and emotional experience? How am I different from my competitors? What can I do to be unique? How can I make the experience paramount and the product secondary?

The answers to these questions are applicable to how you represent your brand online. Make sure you spell out your brand definitively, and be sure to make clear how your brand benefits customers. In addition, personalize your brand. Recall "Mac" from the Apple television campaign? Make one of your own. In other words, your online customers should feel like they're meeting *you* when they visit your site. Remember, perception is crucial. Your web site, as another mode of advertisement, must be consistent with the rest of your brand.

I've been talking about technology as if it's always an arm of advertising. But what about businesses and organizations that are online exclusively? There are many of them. PayPal, the aforementioned eBay, which also owns PayPal; Amazon.com, match.com, eHarmony, iTunes, and CD Baby barely begin to represent the vast number of the Web-only businesses. How could they manage to create a unique, emotional experience? Consider the matchmaking sites, match.com and eHarmony.com. These are sites that promise you, using their technology—their web-based business—will transform your life forever. Using their service, you could change your life forever. How is this possible?

eHarmony is a matchmaking site devoted to marriage. Former Fuller Theological Seminary psychologist, Dr. Neil Clark Warren, and his son-in-law, Greg Forgatch, founded it in 2000. On its Company Overview page, eHarmony claims to be "America's #1 trusted relationship service . . . founded by America's most well known relationship expert, best-selling author, and clinical psychologist." There are several ways in which eHarmony uses technology—its primary platform—to create unique experiences for its customers. Foremost is the nature of the business. It's a business *devoted* to relationships. As such, it is committed to the heart of the brand-building idea.

Of course, the nature of the business does not do all the brand-building work. There are other ingredients. For example, early in the company's history Dr. Warren had strong ties to the conservative Christian community. In addition, he is himself a Christian evangelical and utilizes his expertise as a psychologist and religious thinker in the organization and goal of the online experience. For example, the company is focused on those seeking a long-term relationship and those married couples seeking to strengthen theirs. As a result of the site's orientation, not everyone who applies to eHarmony is accepted. Moreover, not all people seeking long-term relationships are accepted. For example, same-sex couples are not matched, according to Dr. Warren, because same-sex marriages are illegal in most states.

People who are still married, have at least three previous failed marriages, are under age twenty-one, or suffer from severe depression are also those who, according to Warren, will have trouble finding a match. That's because, according to the site, Dr. Warren has done exhaustive research on "what makes marriages succeed and fail." He concluded that there are "29 key dimensions that help predict great relationships."

eHarmony is a prime example of a brand being what it is and not pretending to be something else. "But," you might ask, "isn't eHarmony focusing only on its core customer to the exclusion of others?" No. And here's why. Screening applicants is not the same as doing market research to determine who your core customers are. Moreover, the very design of the questionnaire signifies the individuality of the experience; if it didn't, it would utterly fail to suggest matches between people! Remember, market research tells you the statistics of your core customer. For example, market research might yield the following: male, mid-thirties, lives in an upscale metropolitan area, and so on. There's *no* individuality in the results of market research. What Warren is doing with eHarmony is producing a brand based on his values. He's not profiling, he's setting out parameters based on core beliefs, not core customers cloned by market data.

Another online relationship and dating web site for adults age eighteen and older is Match.com. Founded in 1995 as one of the first consumer dating sites, Match.com focuses its attention, however, not just on people seeking relationships or seeking to strengthen their marriage, but also on the first step toward a relationship: dating. According to its home page, "Match.com is a diverse, global community of single adults who want to find great dates, make new friends, form romantic relationships or meet life partners." Casting a broader net than eHarmony, Match.com, a publicly traded company, promises that you will "Meet someone special within 6 months or get 6 months free," and boasts "millions of members" worldwide.

The way these two relationship-oriented businesses thrive is due to the specific values and beliefs that permeate all aspects of the online experience and, they hope, extend in the particular encounters potential couples have. Though it's true that, as I mentioned earlier, part of these businesses' brands trade on the nature of the business itself, their unique success depends in large part on how they enlist technology. This latter point is applicable also to other web-based businesses.

eBay, for example, has been an online pioneer since its founding in 1995 by Pierre Omidyar. eBay has not only transformed the ways in which people shop, it's transformed itself into an online clearinghouse for almost anything anyone can think to sell. When Meg Whitman took over as CEO in 1998, she enhanced and extended the eBay brand to its current identity. In the process she has helped her company successfully withstand competition from companies looking to break into the online auction business, companies as strong as Amazon, Yahoo!, and Lycos. The eBay brand is so strong that it has withstood not only competition, but also the dot-com bust and internal problems, such as a 24-hour outage in June 1998 and phony auctions that would have frightened customers off a less successful brand. Whitman has been particularly successful in connecting with eBay customers, from eliciting feedback to keeping them in the loop regarding changes to the site. And it's not just individuals who sign up on eBay to sell collectible items. Companies like Sun Microsystems, IBM, and J.C. Penney are among those that regularly sell their products online.

eBay's success is extraordinary, not only because it survived the implosion of the dot com industry, but also because it has managed to create a lasting brand despite the fact that it's an exclusively online company. What eBay's founder and chairman created and what CEO Meg Whitman developed was a values-based, customer-driven business. In Chapter 5, I discuss Omidyar's community business ethic, referencing a 2001 interview he did with *BusinessWeek* magazine. In that interview, he emphasized the importance of transmitting his values to his customers, and in turn, having them adopt those values and pass them along to new users. In this way, each eBay customer—be they buyer or seller—was initiated into the eBay brand.

Moreover, he is mindful of protecting that brand. "What we do have to be cautious of, as we grow," he tells *BusinessWeek*, "is that our core is the personal trade, because the values are communicated person-to-person." The eBay brand survives and prospers because customers have experiences that reflect the eBay brand, and they pass these experiences on to others.

As much as we at eBay talk about the values and encourage people to live by those values, that's not going to work unless people actually adopt those values. The values are communicated not because somebody reads the Web site and says, "Hey, this is how we want to treat each other, so I'll just starting treating people that way." The values are communicated because that's how they're treated when they first arrive. Each member is passing those values on to the next member. It's little things, like you receive a note that says, "Thanks for your business."

My advertising agency created and owned copyrights on a couple of Internet-based software programs that enhanced existing services we offered to our reseller clients. For example, we developed a program that quickly and efficiently executed a number of time consuming activities, thereby freeing clients up to focus on their brand. Prior to using RCI's program, resellers—independently owned businesses that sell products for another company—had to go through a fairly complicated process to create and monitor their advertising budgets. That's because they received a portion of their budget from the manufacturers of the products they sold. The portion, however, was determined in part by how much of that product the reseller bought. Our software significantly simplified the process, which enhanced the level of service we gave to our clients. What the software did not do was *replace* that service.

The Internet is not the only technology you can use to enhance your brand. How you use your telephone, cell phone, messages on hold and voice mail systems, fax, e-mail, and instant messaging devices is an extension of your brand. Technology should help you streamline your operations, create new opportunities, reach a broader customer base, and reinforce your carefully developed brand. *Effective* use of technology is achieved, in large part, through mastery of your brand. This includes never forgetting that *people* use technology, not the other way around.

For example, most people at some time need prescription medication. The last thing you want to do when you're sick, however, is traipse over to the pharmacy to drop off a prescription and then wait around until it's filled. Nowadays, doctors call in or fax prescriptions to your pharmacy so all you have to do is go pick them up. In addition, pharmacies big and small across the country now use telephone-based systems to expedite the prescription refill process. You call your pharmacy, enter information such as your prescription number and the time you want to pick it up, and then hang up the phone. What the telephone and telephone-based systems don't do is replace the important patient–pharmacist relationship. Enhancing, but not replacing your brand with technology is important because of the incredible rate of speed at which newer technology revolutionizes how we interact. For example, the first cell phones in the 1970s were the size—and felt like the weight—of two bricks joined together. Today, there are phones smaller than the size of an average adult palm and light as a feather. And they're getting even more sophisticated. There are wearable cell phones, such as wristwatches, medallions hung around necklaces, and lapels. The array of combination devices—phone, Web browser, calendar, instant messenger, e-mail—can make anyone feel like James Bond. But just as we feel overwhelmed by the vastness of the Internet, we can feel overwhelmed by what technology allows us to do and by the devices that perform these mind-boggling functions.

Some become so paralyzed by the choices technology offers that they can't move to interact at all. Others get so caught up in the bells and whistles that they forget what's really driving the interaction—people. Rather than meet with a customer, they'll make a phone call. Rather than return a phone call, they'll send an e-mail. Those who rely heavily or even exclusively on voice mail and phone tree systems isolate themselves from customers, thereby precluding opportunities for enacting unique experiences.

Of course, the remedy is not abandoning technology, but harnessing its power to expand and extend your reach of influence. Phone calls, e-mail messages, phone trees, and voice mail do not replace person-to-person experience. When, however, it's simply impossible to have an in-person experience, such as when business is conducted entirely online, the *quality* of the way these technologies are used will make the experience more or less effective—just as it does with web-based businesses. Be sure you return phone calls or acknowledge e-mail messages the same day they're received. Keep phone trees simple. Instead of forcing the customer to press button after button, only to be confronted with yet *another* list of questions to answer, set up your call center more like a house than a maze. Limit the number of transfers your customers have to make before they are connected with a live human being. Don't force the customer to input all sorts of personal and account information *before* reaching a live human being—only to have to offer it all up again when the representative gets on the line. Remember, your technology should be an extension of walking in your customers' shoes! When considering technology in your business or organization—large or small—ask yourself, If I were my customer, what would I love from me? I guarantee you, you would not love endless phone trees, unreturned calls—or to be pestered with business calls. Remember the time before you could sign up on the Do Not Call registry?

Regardless of whether your business is brick and mortar or web-based, remember to use technology to *transcend*, not replace, your brand. In the final analysis, don't let technology be the end of your brand, let it be the beginning of expanding, extending, and sustaining it.

CHAPTER 10

BRINGING IT ALL TOGETHER

Understanding the Roles and Fusion of Advertising and Branding to Create the Ultimate Branding Machine

"THE CIRCUS BARKER: AN ORIGINAL DEMING TAIL"

Once upon a time, a circus came to town. All the children were already excited. After all, they'd seen the posters put up all over town in advance of the circus' arrival. Each poster detailed a different act or curiosity, one more incredible than the last. Then the children saw the train roll in with brightly painted car after car of people and animals. The children watched with wonder as myriad characters walked off the train, many carrying or leading animals the children never even imagined could exist. By the time the circus barker placed megaphone to mouth, the children's excitement was barely contained.

"It's going to be tremendous!" one cried.

"It's going to be stupendous!" another shouted.

"It's going to be delightful!" still another squealed.

"It's going to be sometimes frightful!" a small child quailed.

They all shrieked in unison, "The circus has finally come to town!"

Then the barker's voice boomed. "Step right up! This way to sights and sounds you never thought possible! There are ballet dancing bears and flying monkeys! A lion will swallow a grown man's head! Step right this way to see a lady with two heads! Over there is The Rubber Band Man! Don't forget the most amazing sight of all: The Rat Boy!"

"Could it be true?" the children asked their parents. Without waiting for an answer, they shouted, "It must be!" At once they raced in the direction of The Rat Boy.

"Will he have a snout?" one wondered.

"Maybe beady red eyes?" queried another.

"Large ears that sit on top of his head," declared one.

"He'll have pink paws," another said confidently, "and a long, creepy tail!"

"Yes," they all agreed. "A long, creepy tail!"

Clasping their hands with glee, they pressed in close to the tent advertising The Rat Boy. Soon, the circus barker stood before them. "Are you ready to see The Rat Boy?" he boomed.

"Yes, yes!" the children cried. Of all the curiosities, a living rat boy was the most intriguing.

The circus barker noticed this. "Be prepared for a sight you've never seen," he continued. "This is a little boy, no older than you are yourselves."

The children's mouths dropped open.

"But he is also a rat."

"Does he have a snout?" one child asked.

"And beady eyes?" another chimed in.

"What about ears that sit atop his head?"

"He must have a long, creepy tail," they all insisted.

The circus barker put up his hands to silence the crowd. Then he spoke, his tone hushed and serious. "All that you say is true. But you must be very quiet so you do not scare him. Like all rats, he's timid. You must also not try to talk to him. Like all little boys, he is mischievous, and I am sure he will try to frighten you."

The children all nodded solemnly, and the barker drew back the tent flap so the crowd could enter. There, at the back of the tent, was a crimson stage curtain, faded by time, its velvet crushed from use.

The circus barker walked over to the curtain, and with a flourish pulled it open. There, sitting on a chair, was a boy.

The children pressed in for a closer look. Finally, one said, "That's a *boy*, and *only* a boy. That's not a rat at all."

Another said, "He's wearing a costume that's made of fake fur and fake ears."

Still another said, "His tail is made out of a black rubber hose."

At that discovery, the children went silent. The tail was fake. One child started to cry. Then others followed suit. "You tricked us!" they complained to the circus barker. Worst of all was their disappointment that the boy's "rat" tail was fake. Children love creepy things, and of all the boy's attributes, the tail should have been the creepiest. Instead, it was not only *not* creepy, it was fake. "What a terrible tail!" the children wailed.

Without waiting for more complaints, the circus barker rounded up the children and escorted them out of the tent.

The moral of the story: Don't drive your customers to a flawed service!

Your Brand Is Your Foundation

What comes first, advertising or service? Many companies with great marketing have failed because they drive people to a flawed service. Driving people into a flawed business "unsells" them, and the business is, then, bound to fail. On the other hand, many companies have failed because of poor marketing; the company's good, they have a great product or service, but they're afraid of investing in advertising. So they die the slow death. The answer is that it's not a dichotomy, as the question supposes. It's a fusion. First, however, you have to understand what you do, what you can do, and what makes you different from everyone else. You have to understand your brand, create your own service levels, and then produce an advertising and marketing program that speaks to that, which is sincere, unique, and breaks through the clutter. In short, you've got to do what you say, say what you mean, and then overdeliver!

Now that you understand how marketing and advertising are distinct from branding, and you understand the elements of a successful brand, you're ready to pull them together in practice to create customers for life. You have to be sure that your advertising does not misrepresent your brand, or drive customers to a brand that is flawed. There is a lot of temptation to distort your brand through your ad campaign, or to believe that your advertising will stand in for a real brand identity. That's because there is often a fear that a product or service won't break through the clutter to reach customers. Essentially businesses worry that, unless a circus barker approach to advertising isn't used, customers won't be reached. This worry is not entirely unfounded, but their solution doesn't work.

Whenever a product or service is novel—whenever no one else makes or sells the product or service—the brand is in charge. People who want it have no choice but to buy it. Inevitably, however, competition emerges. Think about when the first cassette recorder came on the scene. The Sony Walkman was a revolutionary change in personal audio players, the first portable device of its kind on the market. It wasn't long after, however, that the market was flooded with other brands. Fast-forward to Apple's introduction of the iPod, a portable mp3 player. Though it still dominates the mp3 player market, there is competition.

Competition means the consumer wins. That's where advertising and marketing enter the picture. It tells people where to find you and why you're better. Creative advertising does cut through the clutter of competition, but when the competition starts cutting prices, companies panic and run ad campaigns that are inconsistent with their brand. In this case, advertising either lies to the consumer, or it cheapens brands.

Increasingly, but not always successfully, companies attempt to break through the clutter by saturating the market. For example, the tie-ins between a film, a fast food chain, and certain products reflect the idea that the consumer should have a complete experience. Pushing the idea even further, some marketers attempt to create an entire culture surrounding a particular product or service. Apple's iPod advertisements are especially effective in this respect. Television commercials depicting male and female silhouettes dancing to well-known songs invite the viewer to insert him or herself into the picture. The iPod is suggested in another television commercial as your own personal theme music generator. Who hasn't imagined music welling in the background during momentous life events, just like in the movies? The Super Bowl is another event that marketers use to advertise—at enormous expense—because they believe their product or service is conducive to, or can piggyback off the Super Bowl culture.

Marketers also capitalize off the idea that the consumer is "in control." Whether shopping online, where a click of the mouse can take you to another store, or browsing multiple brands in the supermarket, the consumer is considered "empowered." The role of advertising, then, is to acknowledge and capitalize on that power. But these approaches are wrongheaded when they lose sight of the brand identity the marketing is meant to highlight.

AVOID DRIVING CUSTOMERS TO A FLAWED SERVICE!

What I'd like to encourage people to do is think past this myopic view and enlarge their ideas about experience so that the ultimate customer experience is not object-person or service-person centered, but *relationship*-centered. When RCI, my advertising agency, grew into a national, multimillion dollar organization that serviced every type of business from Fortune 500 organizations to medium and large corporations, I encouraged companies to rethink their ideas of what advertising and branding are. What I did from the beginning was tell my clients that successful branding is achieved not solely through advertising. In those days, this sort of thinking was progressive, and resulted in renegade and wildly successful branding programs.

It wasn't always easy to make people understand that it

makes no sense to drive customers to a business that does not already have a brand identity in place that welcomes and encourages those customers. You can't figure out what your service is after the fact. You can't put a message out that is not reinforced and transcended by the brand experience. Appearance without substance—advertising, driving people to your business without a powerful brand identity—leads to failure.

Many years ago, I was running advertising for a high-end lighting store. They sold everything from table lamps to chandeliers. After we ran a campaign for the business, highlighting the opening of a new store in Ithaca, New York, I got a call one Saturday morning from the owner of the store, Larry. He was fit to be tied. "Hey, Deming," he blustered. "What the $^&# is wrong with the people in this town?"

Immediately, I panicked. The ads had been running for three days, and I thought maybe no one was coming to the new store. "What is it? Aren't there people in the store?"

"Yeah, they're here. Lots of 'em. The store's packed. The place is flooded with people."

With a sigh of relief, I asked, "Okay, so what's the problem?"

"They're not buying squat."

I said, "The place is crowded but nobody's buying?"

He responded angrily, "Right. What's wrong with these people?"

"Larry," I said. "This can wait. The store's full. Let me call you on Monday. I'll come to the store, and we'll talk."

Monday rolled around, and I decided to head over to the new store. "I'm just going to mill around a little, take a look at some things," I told him. Really, I wanted to see how he and his staff interacted with customers. It wasn't long before I learned why there were no sales.

A couple came in looking for a chandelier. They found one they liked—a potential $20,000 sale. "We want this chandelier, and we're willing to pay cash. Can we get a deal, since we're paying cash?" the potential customer asked.

Without batting an eye, Larry practically bellowed, "Discount? Does this look like a friggin' Kmart to you? If you want a discount, go somewhere they sell cheap lighting."

So they did.

After they had walked out, I went over to Larry. "Hey, I think I may have spotted your problem."

"Oh, yeah?" he said, eager to get some business going. "What's that?"

"It's *you*." I paused a moment to let this revelation sink in. Then I continued. "Not only did you lose a $20,000 sale, this man's going to tell *everyone* in Ithaca not to come here. You had a chance for a great sale, even if you threw out 5 or 10 percent, and you would have generated great word of mouth." I knew that Larry was one of those who believed that advertising equals sales. That's why he called me on a Saturday morning. He thought the ads I created weren't getting people to buy, not realizing that the sole purpose of advertising is to generate awareness, interest, and desire to go see what the business is all about. Once in the store, the branding process takes over. Unfortunately for Larry, advertising does not make sales, and it does not make evangelicals.

The brand promise (advertising) has to be in line with brand over delivery. Once you create service levels that rise to the level of creating brand evangelists, you won't even need advertising. In other words, the more evangelists you have, the less you have to do to create awareness. Recall the amazing Costco story in Chapter 4, which addresses this point.

You, with your values and sincerity, are your brand. Until you create a network of evangelicals who do your advertising for you, you've got to get them to your place of business. That's where advertising comes in. Be unique and cut through the clutter, but be sure your ad is consistent with your brand. You must be sure that your marketing strategy is not used in place of a brand identity, nor is it used in an attempt to create a brand. Your brand can only be created by you and the relationships you develop. Do what you say, say what you mean, and always *over*deliver on your brand promise!

CONCLUSION

The paradigm shift I have articulated in these pages is, ultimately, personal for each of us, whether we're the CEO of a Fortune 500 company, or a high school senior making her college applications. The lessons in this book are profoundly simple, and they all lead to one mission critical conclusion: If you want to be successful, you must build a powerful emotional brand. Whether it's personal or professional, you can't succeed in life without a powerful emotional brand. And there's only one way to build your powerful emotional brand, by authentically creating the ultimate customer experience.

In each chapter, my intention is to articulate an element of brands and the brand-building process. But what's most important is that you understand the significance of creating relationships. Whether you're dealing with your family, your friends, acquaintances, customers, employees, or strangers, sincere interactions should transcend anything you promise. What I am advocating in these pages is a guide to integrating aspects of your life into a value-based whole. You are not a separate person in your dealings with your family or friends, customers or strangers. Everything you do reflects what you value—it's your brand. And each part of your brand is inextricably related to the whole.

CONCLUSION

Crucial to understanding and developing your brand is rethinking what you used to believe about a brand. Even if you've never given much thought to it, you've heard the word "brand," and you most likely believe it has something to do with products. If, on the other hand, you are a businessperson or marketing professional, you most likely believe it has to do with either the customer's familiarity with a company name, service, or product, or with manipulating the customer's emotional connection to a product or service. A brand, however, is distinct from both marketing and marketing's tool, advertising. By rethinking the concept, you reorient your thinking toward a new paradigm of branding.

Once you understand this distinction, you can focus on the new model of a brand. This is the second step of the paradigm shift. A successful brand is one that overdelivers on its promise to create a surprisingly unique, memorable, and emotional experience for the customer. What's implicit in this articulation is that a brand is about individual, person-to-person relationships.

In order to understand what this sort of relationship involves, you have to understand the distinction between three types of experience: transactional, typical service, and unique and exceptional. A successful brand transcends the transactional and typical service experiences. Transactional experiences are mere exchanges of money for a product, while typical service experiences simply give the customer what he or she expects.

Once you begin to think about how to create the ultimate customer experience, you are on your way toward creating a sustainable brand and creating brand evangelists of your customers. A customer's perception of your brand depends on the sort of experience he or she has. This experience contributes to building a relationship between you—your brand—and your customer.

In order to create the ultimate customer experience, you must understand what it means to "walk in your customers'—and employees'—shoes." Figuring out what your customers and employees would love from you is an essential component of creating the unique, one-of-a-kind emotional experiences that establish your brand and generate the sort of brand evangelicals that help you sustain your brand. In particular, it involves changing your perspective from viewing customers as opportunities for sales to viewing them as opportunities for new, individual relationships. This perspective change is essential to "walking in your customers'—and employees' —shoes."

Some find it difficult to adopt the requisite position. They think they're already doing everything right. However, "we're not as good as we think we are." This is a difficult, albeit necessary realization on the path toward creating a successful, sustainable brand. Your brand can be made or broken by customers who love or hate you. That's because your customers will praise you to the skies or warn everyone they meet about you. So it's imperative that you pay attention to the individual relationships at the heart of any brand. After all, you never know how your brand will ripple outward.

Implicit in the foregoing discussions is the origin of your brand: you. Everyone is a brand, and everyone needs to understand what theirs is. The successful brand, the one that authentically reaches out to each and every customer, comes from you and your values and beliefs. Once you do this, you can begin to think about how things like technology can be used to enhance your brand—without thinking it will replace it.

Conclusion

What I hope to have demonstrated in these pages, and the concept that emerges at the end of this book, is a complete picture of what a brand is and how it works. When we look at a brand from the standpoint of the whole, we can see the concept of a brand in all of its facets. We can see how the elements of a brand and the process of building it fit together to form a complete account of you and your meaningful relationships—in short, to show you that you *are* your brand!

BIBLIOGRAPHY

BOOKS

Austin, J. L. *How to Do Things with Words*. 2nd ed. Cambridge, MA: Harvard University Press, 2006.

Beckwith, Harry. *Selling the Invisible: A Field Guide to Modern Marketing*. New York: Warner Business Books, 1997.

Cohen, Ben, and Jerry Greenfield. *Double Dip: Lead with Your Values and Make Money*. New York: Simon & Schuster, 1997.

Herbold, Bob. *Fiefdom Syndrome*. New York: Random House, 2004.

Pine, B. Joseph, and James H. Gilmore. *The Experience Economy: Work is Theater & Every Business a Stage*. Cambridge, MA: Harvard Business School Press, 1999.

Myers, David. *Social Psychology*. 5th ed. New York: Worth Publications, 1997.

Schwartz, Barry. *The Paradox of Choice: Why More Is Less*. New York: Ecco Press, 2004.

MAGAZINES (Unless otherwise noted by a particular issue, the following are general references to a magazine.)

Advertising Age.

BusinessWeek. Holmes, Stanley, and Wendy Zellner. "Q&A with eBay's Pierre Omidyar." (December 3, 2001); "The Costco

Way." (April 12, 2004); Rodriguez, Diego. "Saturn's Rust-Proof Brand." (October 21, 2005).

Fortune.

Information Week (April 11, 2005).

Journal of Personality and Social Psychology.

The New Yorker. Remnick, David. "The Wanderer." (September 9, 2006).

STUDIES

"The Retail Customer Dissatisfaction Study" (from "Beware of Dissatisfied Customers: They Like to Blab," in Knowledge@ Wharton, March 8, 2006).

Cannell, Dr. John. "Nationally Normed Elementary Achievement Testing in America's Public Schools: How All Fifty States Are above the National Average" (1987).

Iyengar, Sheena S., and Mark R. Lepper. "When Choice Is Demotivating: Can One Desire Too Much of a Good Thing?" (2000): 995–1,006.

NEWSPAPER AND INTERNET ARTICLES

"G.M. Closings Surprise Perot" (*New York Times*, November 7, 1986).

"Red Faces at the Red Cross" (cbsnews.com, July 30, 2002).

Fishman, Charles. "Sanity, Inc." (fastcompany.com, Issue 21, December 1988).

Greenhouse, Steven. "How Costco Became the Anti–Wal-Mart" (*New York Times*, July 17, 2005).

Meyers, William. "Keeping a Gentle Grip on Power" (*U.S. News & World Report*, October 31, 2005).

INTERNET SITES

www.theacsi.org
www.apple.com/quicktime/mac.html
www.benandjerrys.com
www.businessweek.com
www.cbsnews.com
www.cnn.com
www.eharmony.com
www.fastcompany.com
www.google.com
www.knowledge.wharton.upenn.edu
www.match.com
www.marketingpower.com
http://media.putfil.com/AOL-Cancellation
www.peter-drucker.com

TELEVISION

ABC. *20/20* (2006).
ABC. *Good Morning America* (2006).
PBS. "The Persuaders" (in series *Frontline* (2004)).

FILM

A Few Good Men (1992).

INDEX

Index

INDEX

Made in the USA
Lexington, KY
17 January 2012